Writing Lives

Writing Lives

edited by

Irene Staunton

Published by Weaver Press, Box A1922, Avondale, Harare. 2013
<www.weaverpresszimbabwe.com>

Photographs of the authors: Lawrence Hoba, Nevanji Madanhire,
Daniel Mandishona, Chris Mlalazi, Chiedza Musengezi, Sekai
Nzenza (Weaver Press), Tendai Machingaidze (Taku Machingaidze),
Blessing Musariri (Fungaifoto), Fungisayi Sasa (Rumbidzai Sasa).

Cover Design: Design Duo, Harare.
Printed by: <print@rockingrat.com>

ISBN: 978-1-77922-235-0

Contents

Notes about the Authors

Lawrence Hoba was born in 1983 in Masvingo. He is an entrepreneur, literacy promoter and author who studied Tourism and Hospitality Management at the University of Zimbabwe. Hoba's short stories and poetry have appeared in a number of publications including *Zimbablog*, a journal of the Budding Writers Association of Zimbabwe, the *Warwick Review* (2009), *Writing Now* (2005) and *Laughing Now* (2007). His anthology, *The Trek and Other Stories* (2009) was nominated for the NAMA, 2010 and went on to win the ZBPA award for Best Literature in English.

Tendai Huchu is the author of *The Hairdresser of Harare*, which is now translated into German, French and Italian. In 2013 he was awarded a Hawthornden Fellowship and a Sacatar Fellowship in Bahia. His short fiction has appeared in various journals and anthologies around the world. He is currently working on his next novel.

Tendai Machingaidze was born in Harare. She attended Syracuse University in New York, where she obtained a Bachelor of Science degree in Biochemistry, Magna cum Laude. She also holds an MA in Christian Education and a Master of Divinity degree from Southwestern Baptist Theological Seminary in Texas. Her hobbies include dance, travel, and writing.

Nevanji Madanhire, born in 1961, has worked as a journalist since 1990. In 1996 he became Editor-in-Chief of what was then Zimbabwe's only independent newspaper, *The Financial Gazette*. In 1998, he was part of the team that founded *The Daily News*. In 2002, he became the founding editor of *The Business Tribune*, which quickly grew its readership and circulation because of its fierce independence. It was banned in 2004. He then became the country editor of a London-based NGO, the Institute for War and Peace Reporting. There, he built up a team of ten journalists, which gave the world fresh insights into the Zimbabwean crisis. Since January 2010, he has been editor of the weekly Sunday newspaper, *The*

Standard. He has published two books, *Goatsmell*, (1993) and *If the Wind Blew*, (1995). He has published short stories in anthologies such as *Writing Still* (2003), *All Creatures Great and Small* (2006) and *Mazambuko* (2011). He hopes to become a full-time writer when circumstances allow.

Daniel Mandishona is an architect. He was born in Harare in 1959 and brought up by his maternal grandparents in Mbare (then known as Harari township). In 1976 he was expelled from Goromonzi Secondary School. He lived in London from 1977-92. He first studied Graphic Design, then Architecture at the Bartlett School, University College, London. He now has his own practice in Harare. His first short story, 'A Wasted Land' was published in *Contemporary African Short Stories* (1992). A collection of his short stories, *White Gods Black Demons*, was published in 2009.

Christopher Mlalazi is currently Guest Writer of the City of Hanover in Germany, the latest in a series of writing fellowships. In 2012, he was a fellow at the Iowa International Writing Program, USA; in 2011, he was Guest Writer at the Nordic Africa Institute in Sweden; and, in 2010, Guest Writer at Villa Aurora, in Los Angeles, USA. Prolific as a prose writer and playwright, in 2008 he was the co-winner of the Oxfam Novib PEN Freedom of Expression Award at the Hague for theatre. In 2009, he was given a NAMA award for his short story collection, *Dancing With Life: Tales From the Township*. He was nominated for another NAMA for his novel *Many Rivers* (2009). In 2010 he won a NAMA for his play *Election Day*. He is is currently working on a new novel, *They Are Coming*, which was longlisted for the 2013 Kwani Manuscript Project award.

Blessing Musariri wishes she could dance like the contestants on, 'So You Think You Can Dance', but she has no memory for routines. So, failing that, she hopes she writes even half as well as she wishes she could dance. It is her dream to write a multi-award-winning work of fiction that will be made into a major motion picture.

Chiedza Musengezi has co-edited compilations of women's voices in: *Women of Resilience* (2000), *Women Writing Africa: The Southern Region* (2003) and *A Tragedy of Lives: Women in Prison in Zimbabwe* (2003). Her short stories and poetry have been anthologised locally and internationally. She taught in Ireland and she currently works for the Legal Resources Foundation in Harare. Chiedza was published in *Writing Still* (2003), *Writing*

Now (2005) and *Women Writing Zimbabwe* (2008).

Sekai Nzenza is a writer and an international development consultant specialising in NGO accountability, health, microenterprise and human rights. She was born in rural Zimbabwe and trained as a nurse at Great Ormond Street in London. She holds a Ph.D. in International Relations from the University of Melbourne, Australia. Her essays, fiction and short stories have been published in a number of newspapers and journals including *The Guardian Weekly* and *The Herald*. Her second novel, *Songs to an African Sunset: A Zimbabwean Story* (1997), presents stories of everyday life and the challenges of poverty in rural Zimbabwe.

Sekai returned to Zimbabwe in 2010. Confronted with the consequences of HIV/AIDS, death and poverty in her village, she and the Village Women's Burial Society formed the Simukai Development Project whose aim is to seek practical sustainable solutions to solving rural poverty.

Fungisayi Sasa lives in England. She has written a children's book, *The Search Head*, and her work has appeared in *Blue-Eyed Boybait, Spilt Milk* magazine, *Wordsetc* and *Writing Free* (2011). Several of her poems have been published by Poetry International (Zimbabwe). She is currently working on a short story collection and a novel.

Emmanuel Sigauke grew up in Zimbabwe where he began writing at around age thirteen. He has attempted different genres and has published poetry and short fiction. He resides in Sacramento, California, where he teaches English at Cosumnes River College. He is the founding editor of *Munyori Literary Journal* and is involved in organisations such as the Sacramento Poetry Center and Writers International Network, Zimbabwe, and others. He has co-edited *African Roar*, an annual anthology of short fiction by African writers, a continent-wide initiative.

Our Freedom

Lawrence Hoba

*'It is only in celebrating death that
we can fully understand life.'*

We trudged slowly along, bright early summer stars lighting our way. Meshack, who'd driven us a part of the way, could take us no further. We thanked him, knowing there was nothing more he could do. There was no fuel. We'd spent two hours with him trying to find the twenty litres needed to go *kumusha* and then come back to town; we'd only managed to find five, and these we'd had to drain from another car. It was a bad time to die, and our Freedom had chosen to do just that.

Dzika led us, sometimes stopping abruptly without saying why, sometimes trotting, sometimes shaking his head or murmuring, *'saka Freedom hakuchina'*. We all followed him, he knew the short cuts better than any of us. Later, he would recount how he'd led the way that day, and how we wouldn't have made it to Freedom's funeral without his help; he told the story with such fervour that one could think he'd been carrying us on his back. That was Dzika: but for all his boasting, we liked him and so we just responded, *'zvakaoma shuwa'*.

We didn't speak much on the way. Freedom hadn't spoken much either to give us memories of how sweet he'd been in his short life. But that night, carrying nothing but a few heads of cabbage and a packet of salt, and knowing that food was even scarcer where we were going, I

1

began to think back over everything. Surely, it would have been better for us if Freedom had been stillborn – or shown some sign of weakness or deformity at birth. Then, we could have done something, anything, to ensure that Freedom survived. Things were still good for us at the time. And, as we say, *nyoka dzanga dzichakavburika*. And my brother was still alive. They could have tried again.

Yet, no one knew or could have known that anything was wrong with him that early. How could we have suspected anything, when the elders, who saw him first, came back to us with nothing but admiration? Even the women, who saw him emerging from his mother's womb, the placenta not quite off him yet, had gasped at his beauty. *Gogo* had insisted the baby would not be born in a 'foreign' hospital: that was what had caused the birth of *'vakadzi vese ava* and no man at all,' she said. There were things she wanted to do. Things only she and other elders knew how to do. They would make Freedom a strong man who would outlive us all. We trusted them. Why wouldn't we?

Because, when Freedom was born, he was everything we'd been waiting for. We called him 'our Freedom' because he arrived at a time when everyone said that freedom was dying. But, we claimed, that was their freedom, not ours. Ours was a beacon who would carry the family's name and hopes into the future; the first boy of his generation to carry the clan's name forward. He'd given us the freedom from our worries of extinction. What did it matter that all around us other freedoms were crumbling?

Our Freedom was born smiling. We were living in the army camp then, so we had no idea what the hell those freedom criers were grumbling about. We were used to night curfews, we always carried our IDs, we could not forget who we were and enjoy ourselves without being reminded of the Base Warrant Officer. We envied those who lived outside the camp and their grumbling made no sense to us.

The camp was no one's home. It was just a place where we lived and worked, knowing that one day we would have to leave. Except for a few, none knew when and how this would be. There were many reasons people left the camp. Some were sent to other camps, some retired and some were chased out for one form of indiscipline or another. But one thing that never happened in those days was that people resigned. It was just unheard of.

Only the temporary placement soldiers knew when they would leave. And, since none brought their families with them and they all stayed in the singles' quarters without thought of separating the males from the females, they pretty much threw all caution to the wind and enjoyed themselves, making easy lay of the many young women in the camp, not to mention the occasional married woman. So they filled the outpatients department of the camp hospital wanting treatment for syphilis, gonorrhoea and common fist wounds. Then, they left as quietly and quickly as they came, taking the short stroll from their residence to the parade area where the transport to their next destination awaited them, rucksacks on their backs and canteens dangling from their hands, just as they had when they first appeared.

However, the most common reason people left the camp was death. Soldiers were dying *en masse*. My brother Piki did not escape. After he'd returned from a temporary placement at the Buffalo Range Camp, we neither asked him what he'd done, nor did we look him in the eye, but I knew he'd changed. If he had anything to tell us, he did not volunteer to do so. We buried him in that silence when our Freedom was three, and just beginning to talk properly.

So, we moved closer to home. Freedom would stay with his mother and *gogo* in the rurals. It was cheaper for everyone this way. Life was no longer the same. We could not afford many things. Dzika and I would live in town, and look for work. Living in the ghetto brought us closer to the refrain, 'Freedom is dying!' but we were too taken up with adjusting to our new struggle to notice much; if it had taken them twenty years to realise theirs was a freedom born dying, we had less time.

No sooner had we settled, than our Freedom's mother succumbed to that which we did not know. That was when we should have been worried, but how could we be when our Freedom was well and a bouncing little boy. So we buried her next to her husband's fresh grave and carried on. Our Freedom was alive.

When, a year later, *gogo* called us again without telling us why, we went without premonition. After an impatient silence, we heard her say:

'Something is wrong with our Freedom.' We turned to look at the five-year-old hope and realised in our blindness that it was true. That which afflicted our Freedom had been deceptive; an illness that did not show itself at first, choosing to do so only when it was too advanced for us to do anything about it.

It was the doctor who told us that he'd been born with that silent corruption. Our Freedom had never been free and had lived in the captivity of that which afflicted him from birth. But even as we knew he was dying, he kept smiling, pulling at *gogo's* skirts and never failing to remind us why we had thought he was our freedom. But he had grown thinner and talked less. It was as if he'd learnt a new language that was called silence.

And as I waited in the queue at the government clinic in town, jostling for the medication that would keep him alive, it was only his smile that kept me there for hours on end. In the beginning the queues were not too long and we were asked fewer questions. But as the weeks passed, they grew longer, the interrogation increased, and sometimes I would not be given anything for weeks in a row.

And sometimes, a neighbour or relative came from home and told us how our Freedom was doing and it was always worse than the time before. The calls from *gogo* grew more frequent, more desperate, while the day-to-day situation also grew worse. Everywhere I walked, I heard people say, 'Freedom is dying!' and I would turn, my face growing pale, not knowing if they meant our Freedom or theirs. And every evening, when we knew no one was listening, while eating a plate of sadza and plain vegetables, and knowing I had not received that week's medication, Dzika and I would acknowledge that 'Our Freedom is dying.'

We had begun to hear of people being arrested for saying as much in the streets. We did not want to be caught offside. Yet I could not ignore it and knew, for the first time, that we had become one. Their calls became our calls, our whispers became theirs. We could not speak the words aloud without thinking who might be listening, and they could no longer speak without knowing they would hurt us. Somehow, we were beginning to speak one language and with growing loudness.

We had been rejoicing that I had finally managed to obtain a month's supply of medication when the call from *gogo* came. We had to make it that very night, she'd said. The corpse would not last another day without being buried. So, as we made the final lap, before our homestead, I knew this was our own walk for our Freedom even as we were going to bury him. Already, we could hear the loudest of mourners, probably some new arrivals, making those wailing sounds I'd always hated. I felt sorry for Baba Tino who I knew would be the one to fashion the makeshift coffin from a broken door or wardrobe because we had not bought one and we could not afford to pay the village carpenter. I felt sorry for Dzika … he kept murmuring; *'saka Freedom hakuchina?'* No one answered.

The Life After

Tendai Huchu

A few hours after I crossed over, I still remembered a few things from my former life. I'd not yet drunk the waters of the Lethe. I remembered my father and mama weeping, my friends, family, and everyone I knew and loved, gathered around me. Their wave of emotion, mostly grief, longing, and a sense of loss washed over me. In this state, I could already tell which souls were making the crossing with me and who was staying behind. I was still in the zone between my former life and the life thereafter.

If only I could have held them all a little closer and told them that I loved them a little louder. I should have said that I would come back from time to time, to look in on them, and see how they were doing. This was not the end. But I didn't, Charon was waiting, and I disentangled myself from their embrace, steeled myself against their tears, gave Charon my stub, and was swept away on his vessel, where they could not join me.

I knew that although I was leaving, and the desire to stay was strong, those I loved knew that life had become too painful for me there. It was time for us to let go of what we knew, of the physical, terrestrial bonds that tied us. It was time for me to move on. I was not certain of what lay beyond. Is anyone ever? All I had to count on was hearsay, overheard conversations, glimpses on TV and in art.

I was not alone on my journey. Other souls travelled with me as we were carried up high into the heavens. The piece of earth, which was all I'd known, shrunk and receded from sight, We were pulled ever upwards, watching our homes turn into dolls' houses, the play parks we'd spent our childhoods in vanish, the hills and the valleys we had known disappear, until all that was left was the sky above.

When I was a child, I always dreamed of flying. In my dreams I would soar high above the world, powered by nothing but the strength of my will. Maybe I watched too much Superman and read too many comics, and yet here I was, now, defying gravity and soaring through the sky. My dreams turned into reality at last.

Until then, my life was pretty much unremarkable. I was born into an ordinary family. Father worked for the post office for his whole life, and had risen to the rank of postmaster. Mama was a housewife, and apart from a brief stint as a cleaner, before father plucked her from whatever hotel she worked in, she'd never really done anything else. I was the eldest, and had three sisters who doted on me. We didn't have much, but we were happy.

In telling my story, I wish I could say there had been something more to this life, or that my parents had screwed me up in some meaningful, existential way, but they hadn't. On Fridays, father liked to read to us, after he came home from work. Mama, who couldn't read, would lay her head on his shoulder, her eyes following as he went through the text, almost as though she was reading through him. On Saturdays, he and I went to watch football. Sometimes Tanya, the littlest one, came with us, but more often than not we went alone. I had this feeling of pride, walking with him through the crowds. As he stopped now and again to greet someone, he always told them Pele (that's what he called me) was going to make the local team one day. I did too, and played goalie for four years. He never missed a game, for as long as I played for the team. He'd be drinking a beer with his mates, and you could bet that his face always lit up from the stands when the crowds roared,

'Pele', after I'd made a save. Then, he'd grab the nearest stranger and let them know in no uncertain terms that I was the issue of his loins. On Sundays we always went to church, and sat in the same pew, as a family. That was pretty much it for us. Weekdays rolled by, with father at work, mum at home, and us at school. That was it, week in, week out. We were hobbits, content to be in our own little world until some dark force came upon us. But I rush ahead of myself.

I felt weary as we touched down, and I knew what lay ahead. The other souls looked as tired as I was. Some of them even looked anxious. They say the Prophet Mohammed flew to heaven on a winged steed, Elijah was taken up by a whirlwind, and the Virgin Mary was assumed bodily. I wondered how they felt when they reached their destination. Were they dazed as I was by the bright lights and the press of souls all round trying to get through? Were they confident? Did they know what lay in store?

I was not the only one to feel worried. A bald-headed man took short sharp breaths, as though he'd just finished a sprint race. Beads of perspiration dotted his coconut skull. I envied those among us who looked calm and sure of themselves. We were the ones that had made it across to the other side, the ones who'd left everything behind. Slowly we organised ourselves and began to march forward, shuffling slowly, each weighed down by the baggage we carried towards the inevitable judgement that awaited us. It was a relief to see a child walk by me who carried nothing. Someone, a woman, held her hand as she went past.

Our group trudged on, our feet learning the lay of the new ground. We went as one mass, as though by being together we could somehow have our judgement spread evenly among us. But we knew that when each faced the gatekeeper, they would be completely and utterly alone. The pure among us walked in confidence, the rest of us looked around, searching for a point of escape, a way in that would take us past the gatekeeper. There was none, and so we huddled together and shuffled on.

Though I had left them with tears and grief, I was sure that my people were happy I was gone. You see, life in our little utopia had become unbearable for me. The faces on the others around me showed that I was not the only one who felt this way. Many others had led lives with the same type of pain I'd felt.

When I was at school, I was a rock, suspended high above the earth, full of potential energy. The world was my oyster. They told us that we could be anything we wanted to be, that so long as we applied ourselves, there was no limit to what we could achieve. In my final class of thirty, there were potential doctors, potential astronauts, potential physicists, potential teachers, potential managers, potential entrepreneurs, potential actuaries, potential, potential everywhere.

We were the new generation, the born-frees, those for whom many had paid the ultimate price. Now we were claiming the prize purchased for us in blood, sweat and tears. But when we placed our tokens at the counter, and asked for what was rightfully ours, we were told that the larder was empty, and that while we were in our cots, with our silver spoons tucked in our little mouths, an ogre from the west had come and stolen our inheritance. In the olden days, we would have donned suits of armour, found winged steeds and flown off, steel glistening in the morning sun, to chase the ogre and claim back what was rightfully ours.

There'd been groups of young men who hung around street corners, smoking, and ogling girls on their way to the market. Father called them 'failures', those for whom parents had sacrificed so much and got so little back. The 'failures' were like the seed sown on sandy soil. But these young men were always kind to me, offering a cigarette or a swig of moonshine whenever I passed by. Offers which I always declined. I was sure that I would be different, and that I would not become a 'failure'. I was polite, but stayed away from them. I'd chosen the narrow path, the path lit by books and paved with sharp rocks called hard work.

I was taller than her, when mama lifted me up, after I showed her my A-level result slip with four As. She couldn't read, but she could tell an A from a U, and that was enough. I don't know where she got the strength from, but she held me up there for a very long time, and when she finally let go, I could see the tears of joy streaming down her face. I was dispatched to the post office, to tell my father of my success.

Tanya sensed he might be liberal with his wallet, and came with me. I held her hand as we walked the streets, past the 'failures', and stopping here and there to speak with a friend. We found him in his office, drinking tea and poring over some paperwork. I walked up to him and gave him the results.

His expression was vacant. His finger traced each line he read, as though it was a forensic exercise. When he was satisfied with everything, including the signature at the bottom, he stood up and placed his hands on my shoulders, so we stood face to face.

'We need to discuss your future,' he said.

We found ourselves in a large brightly lit room and joined a long, long queue. I could not count the number of people ahead of me, and those behind me kept increasing. The place felt unnatural and sterile, maybe because it was purely functional. The gatekeeper, our St Peter, was middle aged, clean-shaven, with a hawkish look. My hands trembled, just a minor tremor, as I watched those that came before him. Authority radiated from him, and we all placed our hopes in him. He would look each person in the eye, as though he knew everything, and yet to each one, he asked a series of questions, which I could not hear at the time because I was too far away. Some he let through the gates, others he rejected and told to step aside. Those he rejected were taken away, where to, we knew not.

That was my main fear, to have travelled so far and be turned away. What did I know of the emotions that passed through those who St Peter had rejected? At this point, in the slow-moving queue, I could only empathise, and in my empathy perhaps find some truth of what they went through. But I had myself to worry about, though I'd seen some of these people on our journey, their fate was not bound to mine. Each of us must stand alone and be held to account on his own.

Father and I discussed the future, and we talked about the options open to me. On his salary, with three other children going through school, university was not an option, unless I got a scholarship, and we both knew that without the right connections this was impossible. My hope was to get a job and use my salary to pay for a course at the Open University. He called some of his old connections to see if they had openings, but nothing came up.

I read the newspaper every day, going straight to the classifieds where I looked at the tiny column for vacancies. A scam ran everyday advertising training and work for two hundred till operators. It promised guaranteed employment after a robust course on how to use a till. The other jobs were usually the same, five, ten, fifteen years' experience required. For the first few months, I was eager, sometimes reading the column three or four times just to make sure I wouldn't be left out.

Every fortnight or so, an entry-level position would come up, and I would be filled with hope for a brighter future. I would go to my bedroom, in which I kept my writing materials, and draft an application letter, always starting with, *Dear Sir or Madam*, and ending with, *Yours Faithfully*. Then the waiting would come, weeks of it. I'd hound father, asking whether the guys at the post office had seen anything. He'd always reply that I had to be patient.

I even started applying for jobs I was not qualified for and writing to companies in the directory, on the off chance they had an opening. At least the stamps were free. No one, not one, ever wrote back to me. I couldn't understand it. There I was with my four As, a glittering CV, prefect, chess club captain, debating society secretary, first team soccer player, a number of awards and commendations, and not one company found it fit to hire me. In the solipsism of youth, I did not realise that there were thousands of others, just like me, doing the exact same thing. Too many MCs and not enough mikes.

The football during the weekends kept me sane. There was still a glimmer of hope in my heart, after the first year, and the next. It's hard to explain how your relationship with your folks changes after a stint unemployed, moping about at home, but there are changes. Your requests are now burdensome demands: pocket money – forget it, time spent with your friends is now seen as a waste. Where once you were allowed space and time to roam, now these are indications of how lazy you are. Don't hold it against your folks. It's just that these changes are related to the fact that you're no longer a stone in the sky full of potential; you have become a millstone round their necks, an extra mouth to be fed, a 'failure'.

I began to hang out on the corner with the 'failures'. It didn't happen at once. It started with me saying hullo, and stopping for a chat, just a little longer than I used to, a few extra minutes each day. Then one day, it just happened, and I was one of them. Jimmy, the oldest of us, kept a ballpoint pen tucked in his Afro, and he was sort of our informal leader. We exchanged fantasies about the fast cars we'd one day buy and the hot women we'd bang. These fantasies at least kept us hoping that one day a new day would dawn. Most of the time I just sat at the fringes of the group, listening. Tawanda, who'd finished school eight years previously, was doing his fourth correspondence course in accounting. Mike's girlfriend was pregnant and threatening to tell his parents if he didn't marry her fast. 'Where will I get the money from?' he said, and that was all he had to say about that. For my own part, I was too locked up in my own despair to care about the others. I only came back for the warmth, and the shared commonality of our experience that somehow bound us together.

My feet were sore since our queue's progress was slow. The woman at the front had failed her examination, and was being taken away. There was a separate queue full of whiter souls who were waved in quickly and without much hassle. Our queue was like that of those with the stain of Ham: we had to prove ourselves to enter paradise. Though we had flown together through the sky and across time zones, we were not the same.

The woman in front of me had a rosary gripped tightly in her right hand. She mumbled some prayer, her head bowed. I thought of all the bad things I'd done in my life to see if some karmic effect might impede my progress. The times I refused to help Tanya with her homework. The change I pinched after mama sent me shopping. The lusty thoughts and wet dreams about Miranda, the girl next door. Sins committed through my own fault, in my thoughts and in my words, in what I have done and what I have failed to do. Things that seemed minor then, took on new proportions in the press of the slow-moving queue.

The praying woman reached the front. I watched her, as she was grilled. Where had she come from? Why was she here? He did not take his eyes from hers as he questioned her. I watched her fingers tighten around her rosary. Her answers were slow and hesitant, like an actor who'd forgotten her lines. She tripped, looked confused, repeated herself, and answered questions that weren't asked of her. Then after what must have seemed to be an eternity to her, and moments to me, he shook his head, and told her that she would not be admitted into the Kingdom.

She wept, begged, pleaded, lost all control of herself and fell down onto her knees, her arms outstretched, the rosary dangling from her hand. I could feel the growing anxiety from those behind me. I longed to reach out and touch her, to free her from her abasement, but I was rooted to the spot. Our fates were not intertwined. She sobbed, looking up to him, as if all her dreams and hopes had been crushed. He was impassive, waiting patiently, as if he had seen this too many times and had become hardened to it. Two strong men in identical uniforms came and lifted her up. She did not resist, neither did she help them. Rather, she was resigned, so they took her dead weight between them and dragged her away, taking her to the depths of who knows where.

And so it was that I was called forward, my heart pounding. I shuffled towards him with feet weighed down by lead. Time seemed to slow down, and the gulf between us was great. I could feel his wary eyes studying me, taking in my every step, every motion being of some importance only he understood. If I looked into his eyes or not, that meant something, drooped shoulders, an involuntary twitch in the face, each could be a symbol of my guilt. I noticed a mole on his left cheek that made him seem a just a little more human. Our eyes met. The butterflies fled. My eternity, everything depended on this singular encounter. When I reached his desk I said:

'Good morning, Sir.'

'Passport and landing card,' he replied.

The Red Vienna is Back

Tendai Machingaidze

Driving down Borrowdale Road in a daze, I saw it and smiled. Laughed even, as I was transported back to my childhood. The era of the Red Vienna. Post-Chimurenga. Born Free. Born into prosperity. Born *Takunda*. We had overcome.

I was returning from ten years of studies abroad to visit my parents. I had barely escaped witnessing the crumbling of all my heart held dear. Just before I left Zimbabwe, I had experienced the petrol queues and the rise in prices, but never would I have imagined that in my absence the shops would become a wasteland and my family would rejoice when they managed to acquire a packet of Soya Mince for their dinner and the bargain price of a billion dollars. Though I constantly heard about the daily, and sometimes hourly inflation, and I saw the photos of empty grocery stores, I cannot (or perhaps, will not) comprehend such a Zimbabwe.

My Zimbabwe is the Zimbabwe when the Red Vienna reigned supreme. At parties, at braais, in the tuck shop at school – you were not living if you did not enjoy the tasty goodness of Colcom's Red Viennas. That is the Zimbabwe that is fixed in my soul. The days when the Dairiboard Man was a hero. At the sound of his bell, we would gallop up the street to meet him on his bicycle loaded with a box of ice-cream. Coins jingling in our pockets. Five cents would buy you a Fatso. Twenty cents a Monster Mouse or a Green Mamba. And if you were feeling rich, you could go for a Super Split or a Choc Ice, though never paying more than a dollar.

While I was visiting my parents, I found a five cent coin at the bottom of a drawer. Children today have no idea it is money. They think in USDs. Calculating foreign currency exchange rates has become a necessary skill. Deep down, I long for that little girl with a pom pom in her hair running barefoot down the street to present the Dairiboard Man with a small silver coin bearing a rabbit. I almost threw away the five cent coin I had found. A useless remnant of a lost time. But my mother stopped me. 'I need those to scratch my Buddy Cards to juice my phone.'

As we descended into Harare on my arrival, from my window seat I had watched the red soil and the acacia trees come into focus and in my heart I rejoiced at coming home. How I had missed seeing the city turn lavender with jacarandas in September. And Christmas in May when red bursts of poinsettias peeked through hedges along the streets. Nothing I had seen abroad could match the orange beauty of the flamboyant trees in bloom. As we landed my heart beat once again to an African rhythm. An air of peace filled the cabin as many Zimbabweans exhaled their relief at finally coming home again. But, it was not the same home that we once knew. When I had left Zimbabwe ten years earlier, Harare International Airport was a buzz of activity. Those coming. Those going. Smiles of hullo. And tears of goodbye. A myriad of uniformed staff bearing logos for British Airways, KLM, Lufthansa and the like. Now, I entered a ghost town. Besides the plane I had arrived in, there were no others in sight. None of the shops or restaurants were open. I was greeted by empty spaces and toilets without running water. I was welcomed by desolation and the desperation of those waiting for something nice from America brought to them by the friend of a friend of their cousin-brother who bought it from a sale in Walmart.

My parents did not have enough fuel to come and pick me up from the airport, so I had to take a taxi home. When I asked the driver how much it would cost me to get to Borrowdale, he replied, *'WekuAmerica 150 USD.'* I was clearly not American, but he had seen my bags and heard the accent that had inadvertently slipped into my voice over the past decade and had decided that I was ripe for extortion. Welcome to the new Zimbabwe. I was too dumbfounded to argue so I pulled out the USDs from my wallet and paid the man to take me to a home I knew no longer existed. In the back of a battered Mazda 323 that was masquerading as a taxi, driving down Borrowdale Road I saw the sign. The bright red billboard with five words in block white capitals written across it. 'THE RED VIENNA IS BACK!'

I smiled and the 'taxi' driver who had been eyeing me creepily in the rear-view mirror asked, *'Ko muri kusekei?'* I opened my mouth to answer then realised that I had no words to explain that from the depths of my being, my mind had just been flooded with thoughts of the days when the word 'Diaspora' did not exist in my vocabulary. The days when my friends and I could expect jumping castles and ice-cream cakes at every birthday. The days when Greenwood Park was a wonderland of rides on high chairs and screaming on the train in the tunnel clutching candy floss and popcorn. The days when mothers packed porkpies and crisps for their children's break at school, and Mazoe Orange was a given instead of a national treasure. The days when a black kid from the suburbs could be 'best friends' with a white kid and an Indian kid with no political subtext. The days when...

The Red Vienna is back. But during my brief visit home, I did not rush to TM or Bon Marché to look for it. It is a memory of a Zimbabwe that once was. It will never taste the same again.

Her Books

Nevanji Madanhire

'Why did she die?' we asked ourselves.

She was only 24.

A bee flew into my house the other day. I watched it as it circled the room once, twice, then it made for the window, which was closed.

A bee will behave like the most stupid moth when confronted with glass. Insects will hit their heads against the pane until they drop dead. Even the honey-bee, the smartest insect of them all which lives in the most civilised community, is duped by glass.

After about ten minutes, I opened the window but the bee remained on the pane. I'd imagined that fresh air streaming through the open window would provide it with the necessary cue to a way out, but the insect continued banging its head against the glass. Not wishing to be stung, I took a newspaper and marshalled the insect through the open window and into dizzy freedom.

Would it return to the hive or remain disoriented?

Our funeral cortege slowed down as we approached the steelworks, the residential location, and finally the cemetery that lay beyond. The women, in open trucks, sang the solemn hymns composed for such occasions; the men, crowded into their cars, exchanged dark jokes, as is their wont.

There was comic relief. As my car slowed down, a young cyclist, wearing a white shirt and a pair of stone-washed blue denims with holes in them, as is the fashion these days, was trying to outdo the motorcade, which was not easy on the narrow road. Blinded by his goal, he hit a pothole and fell into a rivulet of sewage. My male passengers guffawed, the female singers shrieked, and the young man picked himself up, crestfallen.

The steelworks were dead. No smoke rose from the chimneys. The few men entering them were hunched figures with stooped heads, like vultures roosting on a tree, waiting to catch the scent of another dying animal.

It didn't use to be like this.

This place was once proudly called 'The Steel-heart of Zimbabwe'. You couldn't miss the signpost as you approached the little town of Redcliff. The steelworkers walked with a bounce. They produced the best steel in Africa, which helped build some of the greatest cities of the world. The town was alive. Goods trains ran on an hourly basis. On their inward journey, they brought in iron ore from mines far away; and on their outward progress took some of the best steel in the world, to nations far afield.

Then, Ziscosteel was the best employer in the country, paying its workers handsomely and proud of their welfare, which it ranked as one of its greatest achievements, and which could be seen in the glow of their children's eyes or the happy laughter of women as they gossiped at club meetings. Now men could no longer look each other in the eye.

'They say No.4 is down again,' one of my passengers commented.

Once it had been the plant's biggest furnace, which the workers proudly called *mabhaira*. Most of the workers were straightforward, simple people who prided themselves as 'the boilers of iron', the ones who boiled rocks and produced molten metal. This was a feat which made them 'real men', and a cut above everyone else. Someone remembered, a worker, a sportsman, who'd run a marathon somewhere in Poland and seen the Ziscosteel insignia on the steel bleachers. 'We made this,' he'd told a Polish competitor, but his pride was all lost in translation.

Beyond the plant, there is a little road to what was once called 'the location' and proudly sign-posted 'Home of the Steelworkers'. There is a small bridge across the river and we could see the rusty water flowing beneath it; the roadside vegetation also a dull rusty red from the smoke spewed by the chimneys of yesteryear.

'*They* have destroyed everything,' another of my passengers said. 'From the best in Africa, to the worst in the world.' I could feel the venom in the way he spat out the word, 'They'.

The residential suburb is called Torwood, or simply Tod. The young call it Karaga, embracing in that single word, their steely lives. Our biker re-emerges: he must have stopped somewhere, to clean up. A small group of men, their heads bowed in respect for their colleague's dead child, are splashed by the cyclist who thoughtlessly rides through another rivulet of waste, having learned nothing from his earlier experience.

'*Mwana whore,* son of a whore!' one of the men hurls an insult at the reprobate. Another flings a stone, and misses. Their anger clearly reaches down to some more fundamental, bottled-up emotion.

But there's still commerce in Torwood. A man, maybe a former steelworker, pushes a cart at the zebra crossing, calling out, '*Mabhodhoro. Mabhodhoro. Mazai apa. Mazai apa.*' A boy of about eight, in a dirty school uniform, emerges from a house, two empty beer bottles in his hands, and exchanges them for four eggs.

As we pass the hospital, we see the ambulance perched on rocks, its wheels long gone, like the laughter of yesterday.

This is the place where she grew up, but in her twentieth year she decided that Torwood was for old people, the luckiest of whom drove 1950s Morris Minors. She went to the city. The rest is the cliché: *Country girl comes to town!*

After her initiation into the city's hurly-burly, she realised, soon enough, that it wasn't for her. Her former lover no longer came to visit her and the rentals on her fifth floor flat were overdue. Her boyfriend said that all his money had been swallowed by the bank, trillions of dollars gone at the stroke of a pen when inflation reached a billion per cent and *they* decided to lop nine zeroes off the currency. Trillionaires woke the following day to find they had only thousands in the bank; billionaires had nothing left. *They* gave such policies a name: casino economics!

The girl looked out over the city. She loved it with a bittersweet kind of love. The glitter. The pain. An ever-evolving form of life in which everyone was an insider living outside. How many times had she felt she'd found a way to survive the city, live it? How many times did such a life slip from under her? She thought of the cars she'd ridden in, the magical places she'd visited, the sweet words the city vultures had heaped upon her as they ravished her youth. And her laughter, which she heard again, amplified by her shame, as it echoed down the metallic corridors of her memory.

But this man had seemed genuine because of the gifts he'd sent to her parents, and because he'd even introduced her to his people. She thought about the car he'd bought for her; it had disappeared recently when he said he was taking it for service.

She was the bee on the window-pane.

She recalled her father's last encounter with the superintendent of the compound, a dapper middle-aged gentleman dressed in a black suit. He came to the house and was offered fearful greetings. The image of her father pleading with him, returned to haunt her.

'I have nowhere to go. This company cannot do this to me. Not after thirty years of loyal service. I was injured *mumabbaira*, in the boilers. Can't they understand that?'

She was in the girls' bedroom, listening, her head bowed in fear.

'I only obey instructions. You have to leave by the end of the month,' the superintendent stood over the father. 'The MD says you have to go. There's nothing I can do about it.'

The father stood up, painfully balancing on the stump, which was all that remained of his leg.

'What about my daughter? If we move out, she won't go to school.'

He limps towards the cupboard in the corner and fumbles as he opens a drawer and pulls out an envelope from which he pulls out a sheaf of paper.

'Look. These are her reports. She will get a bursary next year. But she's finished if you evict us.'

He limps back to the cupboard. 'Look at the trophy she won last year. Best overall student.' He produces a miniature bronze trophy and polishes it against the trouser leg of the stump and thrusts it towards the official.

Is there any way back for the bee?

She opened the window of her flat. A soft breeze drifted in. Sweet? Her nostrils had become inured to the pollution. She smiled wanly. She didn't jump.

They say when a bee senses its own death it doesn't return to the hive.

The graveyard was a godforsaken place, a wasteland on the outskirts of the location. Small groups of people crowded around several new graves. Every week, about ten people were buried in this parched piece of earth. It was not uncommon for several burials to take place at the same time.

The grave had been dug quickly thanks to the spirit of community among the people. The hearse was shepherded towards the grave. The coffin was a cheap one, so people had to hold it at the base rather than by the handles as the body could easily drop though the bottom if the cheap wood could not take the weight. As the men took turns to shovel earth into the grave the women sang the mourning dirges.

She was gone. Dust to dust. A few wilting flowers were placed on the grave; soon enough they would be blown away by the dry winds and only a heap of earth would remain.

People dispersed quickly for there was little food for them. But as they went their various ways, they looked up at the chimneys of the steelworks as if looking for a miracle. Could these giant chimneys once again spew their reddish smoke, as they used to do? That smoke, which poured into their homes was life. They didn't mind if it dirtied their linen, or polluted their lungs. It was their life. For the women it was a sign their men would be going into the *mabhaira* every day and they and their children would live.

'*They* destroyed everything,' people could be heard saying ruefully. 'Is it the curse of our skin?'

They talked about the Germans who set up the plant so many decades ago and ran the plant 'properly'. They talked about the black managers who came after independence and looted the profits, the assets until the plant was brought to its knees.

We went to collect her belongings from the flat. Someone had already moved in – a young woman in her early twenties. She was impatient to know why we hadn't come earlier. Only an entrenched superstition about dead people's belongings had kept her from flinging them through the window. We said nothing. We knew the young woman was merely at the beginning of a new cycle. Soon enough, her people would arrive to collect her belongings.

The room had barely changed. The first thing that struck me was her photograph. It stood on the mantelpiece like a crown. No one has ever explained how the eyes of a portrait will follow you as you move. As I walked about the room, the girl stared at me with a look that was just hers, with its smiling eyes. I wanted to avoid those eyes, so I drew back, but still she stared at me. I returned to the centre of the room, her eyes followed me. What law of physics was this? It was an experience that makes you question everything you've taken for granted.

Most of her possessions were mundane, or so I thought until I saw her books. There were not very many of them, but I was excited to know that she read at all and curious to know what. On top of the pile was a hardback, *Izimpendulo Zika Nkulunkulu*, I wondered where and when she might have learned isiZulu; I didn't remember her speaking, let alone reading, any tongue besides her mother's and English. I tried to figure out the title. Some people call God, Nkulunkulu. *Izimpendulo* could mean answers because there's a similar-sounding Shona word with this meaning.

The next title was Thomas Hardy's *Far from the Madding Crowd*. I picked it up. An old O-level text, perhaps? Something fell out, a bank note. Then I saw many, many banknotes tucked into the book in different denominations. She had been collecting them. They told the story of demise of the country's currency. First there were genuine notes, good money, then came the bearer cheques when the zeroes increased exponentially.

Whom did she wish, at some later time perhaps, to show these notes to, to tell a story, or had it been despair, had she simply given up, as each note became more worthless than the last?

Still, the girl had invested in hope, and I felt my heart twist as I picked up, *A Guide to Family Health*: the cover, a happy family in a swimming pool, the father carrying his son on his shoulders while the mother and the daughter held hands.

The next few, all from the New Lifestyle series, were *Heart to Heart: The Art of Communication*, *Raising Your Child*, and the last had me blinking back tears, *We've Only Just Begun: A Guide to Successful Courtship*. The cover epitomising hope and trust with a young couple looking each other directly in the eyes, holding hands, smiling.

When we'd heard the news of her death, we'd asked, 'Why did she die?'

Now, I felt I knew, she was, like tens of thousands others, a victim of a genocide that history will not record.

Better Build Boys than Repair Men

Daniel Mandishona

September 1968

The funeral wake was at a small house on the southern end of Ardbennie Road, near George Stark School. The dead man's name was Conrad 'Square' Ruwizhi, a notorious robber who had died during a shoot-out with police near the busy flyover on the Beatrice Road. Conrad Ruwizhi's nickname had much to do with his birth, when an inept midwife had deformed the upper part of his cranium into an odd, rectangular shape. On being shown his newborn son, the proud father had asked, 'Why's his head so square?'

And the nickname had stuck.

All the township's well-known criminals were at the funeral – Johnny 'Danger' Machipisa, Solo 'Razor' Kahungu, Christopher 'Violence' Phiri, Elijah 'Mabhini' Nyembe, Eddie 'Sugar' Mushita and the biggest criminal of them all – Innocent 'Godfather' Masaga. The names of these gangsters were scrawled in bright paint on the school walls. Their daring deeds were the subject of hushed conversations in township bars and on the commuter buses. These men were rumoured to possess magical charms which made them immune to bullets.

There were rumours, especially amongst the township's good-time girls, that 'Square's legendary fearlessness was due to the fact that he only had one testicle – a mass of withered and wrinkled tissue that took up half the space in his underwear. Men with a single testicle were supposed to be as fearless as a hundred warriors. It was said that Square, could go to bed with as many as a dozen women at once because of the sexual powers he derived from that single testicle.

Eddie Mushita was known as 'Sugar' because that was what the township girls said he tasted like. Elijah 'Mabhini' Nyembe's nickname had been earned early in his criminal career when he single-handedly hijacked a truck carrying a consignment of plastic rubbish bins. The truck had been found a week later abandoned on the Old Bulawayo Road, minus its consignment of bins and all its tyres. Another criminal, present at the funeral, Innocent 'Godfather' Masaga, was a ruthless extortionist famed for acts of random brutality. People who crossed his path immediately moved their entire families to live in other neighbourhoods, far from Masaga's vengeful tentacles.

Solomon 'Razor' Kahungu earned his nickname after slashing off the ear-lobe of a boy who had made persistent but unwanted advances towards his sister Mary – a busty pre-teen whose promiscuity had earned her the nickname 'Mary Go Round'. Johnny 'Danger' Machipisa was the first township criminal to commit a solo armed bank robbery. At the tender age of seventeen, he had walked into the isolated branch of a large commercial bank and held up the staff at gunpoint before walking out with thousands of dollars bulging in his pockets. The money had been squandered in an orgy of reckless living that had eventually attracted the attention of the police.

He served a ten-year sentence for that crime and because the colonial penal system put emphasis on punishment rather than rehabilitation, he had used his incarceration to become an even more hardened criminal. Later in life, he would become a founder member of the Zimbabwe African Thieves Organisation (ZATO), a loose affiliation of pickpockets, bag-snatchers, loan sharks, burglars and muggers whose sole objective was to emulate the notoriety of the American and Sicilian mafias they admired so much.

It was during the body-viewing ceremony, while the top half of the coffin was opened to allow mourners their last glimpse of the dearly departed soul that Square suddenly sat up, yawned silently, climbed out of his coffin and started walking casually down the street. The mourners who had been lining up to view the body scattered in terror in all directions at this unexpected development. Some of Square's female relatives, including his mother, his eldest sister and three aunts, fainted in a twitching heap in the fierce midday heat.

The hearse, a white Cadillac station wagon from the Heaven Is Waiting Burial Society (motto: *We are the last ones to let you down*) had already reversed into the narrow driveway ready to ferry the coffin to Strachan's Cemetery. As Square walked past, the ashen-faced hearse driver just stared, his toothless mouth agape, his eyeballs nearly popping out of their sockets.

After walking about twenty yards, Square turned back to retrieve his beige trilby hat which had fallen off his chest as he arose out of the coffin. He untangled the red handkerchief tied to the gate (to indicate a death at a house) and used it to dab the sweat off his shiny face. He resumed his journey, walking past the imposing entrance to George Stark School (motto: *Better Build Boys than Repair Men*) and then turned left into Rakgajani Avenue. When he reached the Roman Catholic Church on Ayema Avenue he suddenly quickened his pace. Square knew these meandering streets well, having been born and bred in the Municipality Section's cramped two-roomed asbestos-roofed dwellings.

When not terrorising the God-fearing and law-abiding citizens of the township Square and his notorious crew, the Prohibition gang, would drive around the dusty pot-holed ghetto streets in a 1958 Rambler station wagon dishing out wads of money to beggars and other homeless souls. The gang's vehicle had once been owned by a funeral home in Port Elizabeth and a persistent township rumour was that the car was haunted. Residents claimed to have seen the vehicle on numerous occasions slowly cruising along the streets in the small hours with neither a driver nor passengers in sight. Square's response to these stories was simple and to the point, 'The car is automatic… It doesn't need a driver.'

It had been during a busy month-end Friday afternoon as Square and the Prohibition gang were ambushing a cash-in-transit van that was heading for the heavy industrial area to deliver wages that the notorious hoodlum had met his untimely end. Some of the gang's exploits were more foolhardy than daring; Square couldn't tell the difference between fearlessness and recklessness.

The gang, driving a stolen car with fake number plates, had trailed the cash-in-transit van until it reached a busy junction near the edge of the city centre. As the van pulled up at the intersection the robbers' car rammed it from the side and forced it off the road. Three of the robbers, armed with sawn-off shotguns, alighted and quickly surrounded the vehicle. The men were Conrad 'Square' Ruwizhi, Joe 'Dillinger' Manuwere and Ransom 'Zorro' Masanjala. Unfortunately for them, the police had been tipped off by a confidential informant and were soon on the scene in a convoy of five 'B'-cars, lights flashing and sirens wailing.

In the ensuing confusion the man still in the car had managed to speed off but the three who had surrounded the cash-in-transit van, stranded in no man's land, were left with no option other than to engage the heavily armed police in a bloody shoot-out. Square, who was shot eleven times in the upper chest and three times in the head, died on the spot. 'Dillinger' and 'Zorro' were badly wounded and eventually surrendered near the Nazareth Infectious Diseases Hospital.

As the dead man walked towards Stoddart Hall, a sizable crowd of curious people started following him at a respectable distance. Some daring young boys walked right up to him and attempted to touch him, as if to convince themselves that what they were seeing was really happening – a dead man walking. But Square steadfastly ignored them, striding purposefully towards his unknown destination with both hands insouciantly thrust into his hip pockets.

He walked past the gaudy billboards at Stoddart Hall, casually pausing to glance at the posters advertising that month's 'coming attractions': *One Million Years B.C., Chitty Chitty Bang Bang, Kiss Kiss Kill Kill, Our Man Flint, Five Ashore In Singapore*. Posters of the township's cinematic heroes and heroines were plastered on an adjacent wall – Clint Eastwood, Steve McQueen, James Coburn, Raquel Welch, Sophia Loren, Jane Fonda. The women offered prurience and titillation, the men danger and sophistication.

He walked past the Rialto Nightclub, famous for the ominous warning in the men's toilets: *Anyone Caught Taking Drug Here Will Be Ban Forever*. He walked past a group of Apostolic Faith devotees praying outside the noisy municipal swimming pool, the women long-robed in white, the men bearded, stone-faced and bare-footed. The water in the swimming pool, discoloured with urine, glowed like a fresh oil slick in the mid-afternoon glare. He walked past the fruit and vegetable vendors outside the Community Centre, politely tipping his trilby hat at the astonished women. One of them, recognising Square and realising he was supposed to be dead, wailed uncontrollably as she ran off towards the Number Seven Ground.

At the end of Pazarangu Avenue the dead man turned left into Nyazika Street, past a crumbling roadside kiosk with the sign *We Die Faded Jeans*, past the algae-cloaked public lavatories at the Community Centre that had long been turned into a sleazy gambling den by the glue-sniffers and marijuana peddlers of Sanyanga Street, past the prefabricated and windowless shed that housed the Mother's Love kindergarten school.

He walked past the blighted single-storey structure that had once been a prosperous bakery but which now housed a plethora of unregulated home industries. Amongst them were the Golden Girls Hair Salon, the Mosi-Oa-Tunya Bar and The Ghetto Fabulous Restaurant. He then walked briskly across the intersection of Daniel Street and Chatima Road, past Vito, Zata, Zambe and Jani Streets until he reached Shingirayi Primary School.

By now the crowd following the walking corpse had swelled to about three hundred people, amongst them a pair of uniformed policemen who had been diverted from their usual duties by the commotion. It seemed as though the whole township was now in silent pursuit. The township was known for its strange but well-documented incidents. There was the legendary story of a woman caught by her husband being intimate with an albino baboon on Sondayi Street and another tale of a man who kept a dead python in a metal trunk underneath his bed at the Matapi hostels. But there was no record of a resuscitated corpse. A breathless newcomer soon joined the crowd of followers.

'Who is that man?'

'It's a ghost.'

'Isn't that Square Ruwizhi?'

'So, if you already know who he is, why are you asking?'

'But is he not supposed to be dead? Wasn't he shot by the police at the flyover?'

'He *was* dead. He just woke up.'

'You cannot wake up from death, unless if you are Jesus.'

'Maybe he is Jesus.'

'Don't use the Lord's name in vain, young man.'

'Don't ask stupid questions.'

'So where's he going?'

'Nobody knows. He just got out of his coffin during body-viewing time and started walking.'

'Why don't the police arrest him?'

'Arrest him for what? The guy is already dead.'

At the end of the street the dead man turned left and started walking towards the neat rows of semi-detached houses known as the Beatrice Cottages. By now the crowd in front of him was just as large as that behind him, a seething groundswell of curious faces and excited voices. Square remained resolutely unmoved by the commotion around him.

On Mbirimi Drive he suddenly stopped, and the huge crowd also stopped. He put his hand in the jacket of the black suit he was wearing and pulled out a crumpled packet of Madison cigarettes. But he soon discovered he had no matches. Deceased members of the criminal fraternity were usually buried with those material things that they had cherished during their days on earth, but the undertakers had forgotten to provide Square with a box of matches.

Square had been a big drinker and chain-smoker. On most Friday evenings, after a successful day picking the bulging pockets of the commuters at the Mashonaland Turf Club bus rank on Cameron Street, members of the Prohibition gang were well known for the drinking parties they hosted for their girlfriends at the El Morocco and Bonanza Nightclubs, the two rowdy establishments located at the sleazier end of the city centre. The parties would last all night and on offer to those

privileged to have been invited would be every imaginable intoxicant –
dagga, beer, brandy, port, whisky and wine.

Square turned around, holding out his hand to the crowd as if asking
for a lighter. The people behind him scattered in all directions. It was
the first time most of those walking behind him had actually seen the
dead man's face. There were dark rings around his eyes and both his
nostrils were plugged with wads of cotton wool. It was a hot day, and
a thin lining of sweat covered the corpse's face. Square casually put the
unlit cigarette back into his packet and from his other jacket pocket he
retrieved a quarter bottle of Old Chateau brandy. Unscrewing the top,
he took several long swigs and then nonchalantly put the bottle back
into his pocket.

'Look, he's drinking,' said an excited young boy standing on an up-
turned bin.

'Of course, he's drinking. It's a hot day.'

'But he's dead.'

'Just because he's dead, you think he can't get thirsty?'

At the top of Barbara Tredgold Crescent the dead man turned left and
started walking towards Strachan Cemetery. When he got there he
walked towards the municipal gravediggers who were working on some
new graves. It must have been the sight of the corpse's face, or perhaps
one of the gravediggers recognised the notorious hoodlum, but the men
quickly dropped their tools and scattered, yelling, in all directions.

The dead man casually picked up one of the discarded shovels,
walked to an open grave near the cemetery's small central chapel and
slowly, unperturbed by the scorching heat, started shovelling the mound
of red earth back into the gaping hole. Behind him a metal crucifix sat
on the apex of the chapel roof, eerily surrounded by a radiant halo.

'What's he doing now?'

'That's the grave he is supposed to be buried in...'

'How do you know that?'

'I'm his uncle and I'm the one who paid for it yesterday. I guess he
doesn't want to be buried anymore.'

'But he's dead, he has no choice.'

'Why don't you go and tell him that?'

After filling the grave with gravel, Square pulled out his quarter bottle of Old Chateau and took several more long swigs. He burped loudly, and then tossed the empty bottle into the yawning hole in front of him. Then he turned and started walking back in the direction of the Community Centre. The crowd had by now swollen to over five hundred people, including women with noisy infants strapped on their backs and even an elderly man on crutches. Superstitious, but curious nonetheless, they kept at a respectable distance behind the corpse.

By now, Square's gait had become increasingly disoriented. Perhaps it was the unbearable heat, or maybe it was the Old Chateau. After all, he had been dead nearly three days and was unwisely drinking on an empty stomach, if he had a stomach left. Square was a Moslem (although this didn't stop him drinking) and the Moslems in the township were known to disembowel their dead before burying them. The two uniformed policemen were now walking purposefully about ten yards on either side of the dead man.

'Do you think they're going to arrest him now?'

'Arrest him for what?'

'I don't know. Public drinking – or something like that?'

'Don't be stupid. He's dead. How do you arrest a dead man?'

Square was now unsteady, lurching sideways and even leaning onto the front walls of adjacent houses for support. The two policemen had brought out their handcuffs but still seemed unsure as to what they were supposed to do. One of them was talking into a walkie-talkie but nobody could make out what he was saying. All that could be heard, over and over, were the words 'Roger, over and out, Roger, over and out.'

'I think I know where he's going,' said the uncle who claimed to have paid for the grave.

'You do?'

'Yes. But let's wait and see. It's just around the corner. Let's just wait...'

Sure enough, as the dead man reached a sharp bend on Francis Joseph Street, he walked up to the front door of a small house roofed with discoloured asbestos sheets. Outside the house a hand-written notice on a plywood board notified passers-by that there was an imported wedding gown for hire. Now totally unsteady on his feet, Square held on to the wall with one hand while with the other one he rapped the door three times. There was no response. The crowd, now noticeably tense and expectant, silently surged forward. The dead man rapped on the door again, this time with more urgency.

'So you know who lives there?'

'Yes. Al Capone lives there.'

Norman 'Al Capone' Fernando was a small-time crook who had been unceremoniously expelled from the Prohibition gang for having a very public affair with one of Square's numerous paramours. Rumour had it that it was information supplied by him that had led to the failure of the Prohibition gang's heist and the bloody police ambush on the Beatrice Road flyover bridge.

Then, for the first time, the dead man spoke – an eerie sound that seemed as though it came from the depths of the earth.

'Al Capone, come out now. The time to pay has come.'

The crowd moved back in unison, like the waters of a receding tidal wave.

'It's time, Al... You have to pay.'

A small boy at the front of the crowd laughed and clapped his hands in anticipation.

'Open the door. Come out now. You have to pay.'

The crippled man tried to climb onto a bin and fell over.

'Al Capone, open the door. You have to pay.'

'You have to pay, Al.'

When you opened your eyes Mother towered over you, her hands on her hips. She shook her head as she always did when about to admonish you and sighed despairingly. You tried to open your eyes fully but the sun filtering in through the torn bedroom curtain blinded you, stung your eyes like a whiplash.

'Now that you're dreaming of thieves and hooligans – don't make a face, I heard you talking about that no-good rascal Square Ruwizhi in your sleep just now. Now that you're dreaming of thieves and hooligans, I hope it is not your ambition to become one of them,' she said.

The intense sunlight seemed to be boring tiny holes in your skull.

'The post office opens in five minutes. You have to go and pay your school fees otherwise they won't let you into the class tomorrow. You want to sleep till ten or what? Your friend Al is waiting for you outside.'

Al was Albert Chingwezha, your best friend.

'I'm sorry, Mother. I must have overslept. I was dreaming.'

'You're always dreaming. But you have to go and pay. You know what the queues are like at the post office this time of the year.'

'Sorry Mother, I'm going now.'

'Your friend Al has been waiting outside for ten minutes. Go now...'

She whipped the blanket off your body, exposing your goose-pimpled thighs and the expansive patch of urine you had spent half the night tossing and turning in. And that was how you would always remember mother, as somebody who always disrupted your sleep, as somebody who always stole your dreams.

At the post office you joined a long queue that stretched hundreds of feet into the dazzling sunshine outside the building. There were men, women and children in a queue that included an elderly man on crutches and two uniformed policemen. One of the policemen kept talking into a walkie-talkie: 'Roger, over and out. Roger, over and out...'

The people around you looked vaguely familiar; it was like reliving a past experience. At the front of the queue, in angled trilby hat and immaculate black suit, was the notorious township gangster Conrad Square Ruwizhi, his eyes ringed with the accumulative fatigue caused by his legendary hard living at the Bonanza and El Morocco nightclubs.

Whilst the post office clerk attended to him, Square occasionally took long swigs from the bottle of Old Chateau he kept hidden in the breast pocket of his jacket. Public drinking was not allowed, but who in their right frame of mind would dare arrest Conrad Square Ruwizhi – fraudster, conman, forger, armed robber and the single-testicle leader of the township's notorious Prohibition gang?

Tsano

Christopher Mlalazi

My name is Gubha Jamela. Gubha means to scoop a hole in the ground in Ndebele, and now I'm digging mass graves. Was this my destiny when my parents named me?

Crazy as it seems, I'm happy doing this. People need to be buried. No one needs to be told that. And I'm burying my people. It's the last good thing I can do for them to ensure their souls rest in peace and their progeny lead normal lives. That is, once all this is over.

Even these soldiers – especially those who've maimed and killed – know that when a dead body isn't buried, its soul will roam the earth upsetting the living; this is why I'm now their man with a pick and shovel.

There are still some bodies that haven't been buried, like those I saw from the bus on the last day of my freedom.

The soldiers say they want to wipe out all the Ndebele people. They say the Ndebeles do not belong in Zimbabwe, that their home is in Zululand from where they ran away with their leader Mzilikazi, fleeing the rule of King Tshaka. They say that Zimbabwe belongs to them, the Shona.

And the soldiers aren't joking. No, they're killing everybody – men, women and children, even livestock. They're also burning everything

– homes, fields, granaries – they say, quite openly, that they want to starve to death those they haven't already butchered. And now I'm one of their official gravediggers. There are four of us. Every morning they give us picks and shovels, and every morning at a new site in the forest we dig a grave as wide as a house, and as deep as two men standing on top of each other. At sunset, we fill the hole with the day's murderous harvest. Sometimes, we fill them immediately after a killing – if it's done on site – otherwise the bodies are brought in by army truck like tainted carcasses from a condemned abattoir.

***

I'd heard in the city that soldiers were killing people in the rural areas, but the words didn't convey the horror of it. I'd never seen a murdered corpse lying on the ground before. Yes, at wakes, I'd seen bodies in their coffins but never one lying on the ground with flies hovering over it, or one swollen like a balloon about to burst, or smelling bad, like rotting meat.

***

I'd left the protection of the city to fetch my family from Mbongolo, my village. What else could one do? The village is where we belong. I was born there and my umbilical cord is buried there.

I'd heard that the soldiers were in Tsholotsho, in Matabeleland North, I'd heard the stories that they were killing people like we kill *intethe* in the fields; that they were burning villages, raping women, but I hadn't thought that they'd go to my village of Mbongolo in Matebeleland South, it seemed so far away from Tsholotsho. But now they're here in Mbongolo, and we're disappearing from the face of the earth faster than you can cry, 'Dear Lord, please save us'.

When Mzilikazi, who'd been a commander in Tshaka's army, fled Zululand with his Ndebele people in the nineteenth century, he found people already living here: the Kalanga, the Tonga, the Venda, amongst others. He defeated them, and took their lands, incorporating some of them into his new Kingdom of the Ndebele. Of course, he must've killed some of them – those were the times of *amabutho* and conquest. Then, from his new kingdom, Mzilikazi launched raids into the northern part of the country, and his warriors killed the Shona and took their cattle; he also incorporated some of them into the new Ndebele kingdom. Everyone knows this story. It's in the history books, and even those who did not attend school know it, but it all happened over a century ago.

So, how is it, that now, just three years after Independence, red-bereted Shona soldiers have come to Matabeleland breathing hellfire, and every time they order people to jump into the graves we've dug, some of them scream that they are revenging Mzilikazi's sins, as if that justifies every bullet. Sometimes, we're ordered to bury people who are still alive. The other day one of the gravediggers couldn't take it any longer. He threw away his shovel and jumped into the pit of bodies. The soldiers laughed and pumped him full of bullets from their AK's. We just piled dirt on him too, along with the rest. He was a brave man. I think of doing the same before I go mad, but then I remember my wife and daughter and know I can't die without finding them.

***

When the soldiers were deployed a few months ago, the news on the government radio and in the government newspapers said they were coming to fight the dissidents who were robbing and killing people in the countryside. But when the soldiers arrived, it seems they forgot about the so-called dissidents, and decided to concentrate on the villagers; maybe the dissidents had been the excuse they'd been waiting for to start their conquest – who knows? Whatever, soon there will be no Ndebele people left in the countryside.

***

I'm Ndebele, and my wife Mamvura is Shona, and we've been happy together. Even her people gladly agreed that I, an Ndebele, marry their daughter and they accepted my lobola – but now these soldiers, her people, are saying Ndebele people must be wiped off the earth. We have a fourteen-year-old daughter, Rudo – a Shona name meaning love. Mamvura and I had agreed that if our first child was a girl, we'd give her a name from the female side of the family, and if it was a boy, we'd name from the male side. How will my daughter survive, if she survives, as she is of mixed tribe?

***

When I left the city, I went to the Renkini bus terminus to catch the bus for Mbongolo village. I didn't buy any groceries as I normally do. I usually return home every two months with enough supplies for my family until my next visit. If they need anything before then, they send me a letter with Ndoro, the driver of the Mbongolo bus, and he takes back whatever is needed.

Ndoro is Shona, from Mashonaland East, and he calls me his *tsano*, which is Shona for brother-in-law as my wife comes from the same area though they're not related and did not know each other before they met in Mbongolo. I like Ndoro and he speaks very fluent Ndebele, even better than some Ndebeles I know.

That day at Renkini, Ndoro told me that things were very very bad in the village, and that it would be sensible if I remained in the city, which was safer for me. He said that he would bring my family back with him when he made his return trip the following morning. But I felt I had to go and fetch them myself, and make sure they were safe. I was worried that Ndoro might not find them. I thought they might have run away. I also asked him why he wasn't afraid to drive the bus to and from the village, and he told me there were two reasons the soldiers left him alone – he was Shona and he often brought alcohol for them.

***

The bus left at 11 a.m. It takes six hours to reach Mbongolo. This is because the journey is circuitous, not as the crow flies. It was a hot day. It's the rainy season, but the rains are nowhere in sight. I knew that if it was hot in Bulawayo, it would be worse in Mbongolo, a place, which is fast becoming a desert, like Botwana.

The bus was not full, as it usually is, or was before the soldiers came. And I was the only man on it that day, not counting Ndoro. The rest were old women. Perhaps they felt they had nothing to fear as they were in their twilight years. I counted the women, eleven of them, apparently travelling separately, except for two who sat together. No one talked, we just sat, engrossed in our own thoughts. There was also no conductor. Ndoro collected the fare as we entered the bus at Renkini, and put the money into a leather bag which he'd hung around his neck.

'My conductor ran away, *tsano*,' Ndoro told me as the bus wound its way through the city streets, headed for the countryside. I was sitting two seats behind him. In his fifties, he was dressed in blue overalls and wore a green woolly hat.

As we neared the outskirts of the city, Ndoro told me to come closer to him. 'You know what,' he said, as he took the money bag from around his neck and tossed it to me. 'Take this bag and hang it round your neck. There's a roadblock of soldiers just outside the city and if they ask, tell them you're my conductor. Just stand by the door, like that, I don't want my sister Mamvura to lose Rudo's father.'

And so that day I became my *tsano's* conductor.

At the roadblock, another bus was parked behind two Puma army trucks. All its passengers were lying on the ground in a line by the kerb. Three soldiers were standing amongst them, beating their buttocks hard with sticks, just as one would play a marimba. All the soldiers wore the red berets of the 5th Brigade. There were about twenty of them. An electric fear hit my heart as one of the soldiers walked towards our bus. I looked at Ndoro. He was smiling at the approaching soldier through the windscreen.

'Just take it easy, *tsano*,' Ndoro hissed at me, still smiling. 'I know this son of a bitch.'

I can understand Shona and speak a bit also, although with a rough accent. I like the language, it is full of 'r's and is very descriptive, very musical, especially when my wife speaks it. The term Gukurahundi means 'the first rain that washes away the chaff', which is what the soldiers call their campaign. All these red berets looked to me like giant bloody raindrops, which had fallen on the dry earth of Matebeleland.

The bus rocked as the soldier climbed in. At twenty something, he looked like a child.

'Ndoro, what's happened to your conductor?' asked the soldier, in Shona, glaring at me.

'That thief ran away with the bus money when I reached town last night,' Ndoro responded, still smiling. 'You know these young people, always looking for a score.'

'You see what happens if you trust an Ndebele,' the soldier said.

'Dissidents, all of them, but this time we are sorting them out for good.' His eyes roved over the women in the bus. 'And what kind of a trip is this? How come you've only got these *varoyi*, these witches here?'

'Just some old women going back home.' Ndoro said. 'You know old people belong in the villages, the cities are for the young.'

'Are you sure these are not dissidents pretending to be old women?' The soldier pointed at one of the old women sitting three rows away from the door. 'You, stand up!' he barked at her. The old woman did not stand, but looked at the soldier, baffled. 'Don't you have ears you witch, I said stand up!'

'He's saying "stand up", *Gogo*.' Ndoro translated for the old woman.

'Why should I stand up?' the old woman asked in a quavering voice. 'Does he want to kill me too?'

'What did that *muroyi* say?' The soldier demanded. He stared at the old woman. 'Don't speak your Ndebele filth to me! Stand up now before I shoot you.'

'Please stand up, *Gogo*,' Ndoro interjected quickly. 'If you don't you'll be killed. You know these people yourself and what they do.'

The old woman wobbled to her feet, and the soldier approached her, grabbed her blouse and tore it off, leaving her breasts exposed. I closed my eyes. I heard the soldier snickering. Outside the bus somebody started screaming, and the heavy sound of blows on bodies filled the bus.

'If you try to be funny, I can take you off the bus and cut your vagina open.' I heard the soldier saying, and opened my eyes. The old woman was standing naked from the waist up in front of the young soldier, trying to cover her breasts with shaking hands. Then the soldier threw her blouse over her head in a dismissive gesture, and glared at the other women. Once more an intense silence fell inside the bus. Outside, many people were screaming, and there were sharp shouts in Shona, and the sounds of more blows. I dared not look in that direction, fearing that if I was seen doing so, I would not continue with this journey. I stole a quick glance at Ndoro. His bearded face was inscrutable, as he stared straight ahead. I saw this was how he survived.

The soldier suddenly looked at me. My heart lurched. But he did not say anything, and he looked again at Ndoro. The glare had gone from underneath the red beret, and he smiled.

'Good, we need all the old women to go into the villages and weep for their children,' the soldier said. 'We mean business. They haven't seen anything yet. We're going to drink their blood until they're as dry as sticks.'

Thankfully, and with that, the soldier left the bus, and we breathed again as we continued with our journey into the heart of madness.

***

'Sin.' Ndoro muttered as the bus continued on its journey, thundering into the countryside. 'Madness.' I could see that he was not speaking to me, but to himself. He kept repeating the word 'madness' as the bus moved along. We'd now left the tarred road for the dust one for that would take us on the circuitous route around the Matopo Hills. 'It's not the Shona people who want this,' Ndoro muttered. 'They're lying. This is politics.' I kept my mouth shut.

There's no sight that can inspire as the Matopo Hills. The shrine of Njelele is found here, a proof of the spirituality of these hills. The first Ndebele King, Mzilikazi, is buried here, and so too Cecil John Rhodes, that white man who broke the Ndebele Empire under Mzilikazi's son, King Lobengula, with the Gatling gun. Considering the beauty of these hills, one would think a force would arise from the rocks to overwhelm the soldiers and their masters as punishment for their sins, so that they become as maggots on the ground.

'Sin,' Ndoro kept muttering. 'This will kill our new nation and divide our people. I'm a full Shona and I don't see why Ndebele people should suffer like this. This is politics at its worst. They just want to break ZAPU.'

We arrived at Nkwalini shopping centre at three in the afternoon. The sun was still high, and still hot. As we approached the shopping centre, and the bus stop, marked by an *ntenjane* tree with the sign 'Nkwalini' nailed to it at head height, I saw a heap of something that looked like logs. Then, I recoiled in horror.

The logs were corpses, swollen to the point of explosion. A dog was tearing at the foot of one of them. All were naked. The bus stop sign had been scrawled over with the words 'DISSIDENTS' in red paint. Ndoro cursed under his breath and drove past the tree, stopping beyond it. There was nobody at the bus stop, but the old woman with the torn blouse hobbled off, an old green towel wrapped around her upper body. I stared down at the pavement. Some soldiers carrying bottles of beer were pointing at Ndoro and laughing. Then two of them came towards the bus. A smell of rotting flesh invaded the bus.

The soldiers looked up at Ndoro through the driver's window. Both had shiny, sweaty faces and seemed drunk.

'You see, Ndebeles,' one of the soldiers said to Ndoro, pointing with his bottle at the corpses. 'They make good food for dogs.' The two soldiers laughed. I looked at Ndoro. He took a bottle of Mainstay from a box beside his seat, and passed it through the window to the soldier who had spoken.

'Good man,' the second soldier said. 'You're the bus driver, a true Shona who knows his brothers need their drink.' The soldiers walked back to the pavement. Ndoro had not uttered a word.

We continued with the journey. I felt like vomiting, I could barely hold the bile in. A soft keening came from one of the women in the bus, and when I looked at her, she had her face buried in the bosom of the woman sitting next to her, her shoulders heaving. The other woman's face was covered with her hands.

'Oh God!' I prayed that my family was safe.

'I told you to remain in the city, *tsano*, now look at what you're seeing,' Ndoro said to me.

'I have to fetch my family,' I replied, my voice almost breaking.

'And die in the process? You're safe in this bus, but once I drop you off, you're on your own. I shan't be able to help you.'

***

We arrived in Mbongolo at five in the afternoon. My stop was fifteen minutes beyond it. Chief Mabhena's homestead lies in between and is visible from the road. A Puma truck was parked outside his home. There was activity around one of the huts in the compound. About ten people were being herded into it by the red-bereted soldiers. Mabhena has two wives and many children, one of them Nobuhle, is my daughter's classmate and best friend. A soldier with a club was beating people into the hut, like cattle into a pen. I clearly saw Mabhena from his shock of white hair. He was carrying a baby. A club in the hands of a soldier kept descending on his shoulders again and yet again. I imagined the sound of those blows. Then the baby dropped from Mabhena's hands, he knelt down to pick it up, and a booted foot kicked the baby like a ball through the door and into the hut. Then the club landed into the back of Mabhena's head and he collapsed to the ground. Two soldiers, holding him by hands and feet, swung him into the hut like a meal-ie-meal sack and closed the door.

The soldiers then set fire to the roof of the hut. The door imme-diately burst open and a woman emerged clutching a baby to her bo-som. Her mouth was open in a soundless scream. There was the crack-ing sound of gunfire and she fell back into the hut. A soldier closed the door again, and then two of them rolled a large stone against it. The roof of the hut was burning fiercely. I could imagine the screams, imagine their bodies burning inside the hut; but, the bus was still a short distance from Mabhena's homestead, and no sound reached us except that of gunfire.

'This is why there's a drought in Matebeleland,' Ndoro muttered as the bus roared past the burning dwellings. 'It's a portent, trust me.' The soldiers looked at the bus impassively as it passed. Some of them were now setting fire to the other huts in the compound.

'Sin. Sin!' Ndoro muttered, shaking his head, as if to rid himself of demons. 'The North Koreans who trained these soldiers to become such monsters will pay for this one day. The world does not forget, and it is waiting.'

***

A few minutes later, we approached my bus stop. My heart was in my mouth. Behind us, I could see a plume of smoke writhing into the sky from the direction of the Mabhena homestead, and I could hear the sound of rapid gunfire, although I did not know where it was coming from, and who was being shot at.

***

My bus stop is a tree by the side of the road on which is tied a metal sign, 'Jamela Bus Stop'. My home lies behind a hillock beyond the bus stop. It cannot be seen from the road.

42

I heard Ndoro whistle under his breath as we rounded the bend. Nearest to the stop is my brother Genesis's home; he's the eldest in my family. It had been reduced to ashes from which a little smoke wafted. A pile of what I assumed were burnt bodies lay in what had been the kitchen hut. They must have huddled together before the flames reached them.

I did not see myself leap from the bus.

'Come back *Baba va*Rudo!' I heard Ndoro shouting as I ran past Genesis's home. To the left was my second brother's home, Francis. His homestead was similarly reduced. Later I knew that his family had perished in the bedroom hut where their bodies formed a charred lump in the middle of the floor. I threw the bus driver's money bag behind me as I ran. I rounded the hillock that hides my home from the road, and collapsed on my knees. My home was standing, not burnt. It stood there beside the big *mopane* tree at the gate, three huts surrounded by a wooden fence. The soldiers must have missed it, hidden as it was from the road. My heart lightened. I raced into the yard, but it was deserted. I called out my wife's name, my daughter's name, but there was no reply. I ran to the bedroom. It was empty. And so were the other two rooms, the kitchen and the spare bedroom. Oh God, my heart sank, maybe they'd died in one of my uncle's homes. Then I heard a hiss. I was standing in the middle of the yard. The sound came again, it was above me; no, it came from behind. My heart stood still. I looked again, and felt as if the earth was going to swallow me up. It was a soldier. He was standing beside a tree in the bushes outside the fence. As soon as I noticed him, several other soldiers stepped into the open. They advanced towards me. They all wore red berets.

***

'Hullo dissident,' one of the soldiers said when they came up to me. 'We've been waiting for a very long time for somebody to appear here.' He was speaking in Shona.

'I'm not a dissident,' I replied. 'This is my home and I've just come from the city where I work.' The Ndebele accent in my Shona sounded like boulders rolling down a hill that day.

The soldiers did not listen. I was tortured in my yard until the sun returned to its mother. I was made to run in circles with my pointing finger on the ground, and when I became dizzy and fell down, I was made to roll around in the yard while one soldier poured water over me with a bucket and another beat me all over the body with a club. Then they took off my clothes, and one of the soldiers brought one of my donkeys from the kraal. With a noose around its head, they tied it to the *mopane* tree, and said I must mount it. A soldier brought a chair for me to stand on and tied a length of elastic around my penis, and the other end to one of the fence posts. They pushed me back, stretching the elastic and my penis; then a soldier whipped my penis with a thin stick while another one repeatedly hit me on the head with a club. Finally, I lost consciousness. When I came to the following morning, I was inside the barbed wire fence in the middle of the Mbongolo primary school grounds, which was full of people. My penis was throbbing and swollen. At around ten they gave me a pick and a shovel, and with other men, they herded us into a truck and drove us into the bush, where I dug my first grave. When we'd finished the hole, the truck left, returning a while later with all the people who had been captive at the school: men, women and children. They were made to stand at the lip of the pit, and then they were sprayed with bullets by the soldiers who stood behind them. Most fell into the pit, and we were made to throw in the few who fell outside. Thirty-two were killed on that first day. We filled the grave with soil immediately afterwards. Some of the people were still moving as we did so. I had no choice but to get on with the work. I wanted to live. Maybe, one day I can escape to look for my wife and daughter, and if they are dead, bury them properly so their souls can rest peacefully with our ancestors.

I've been behind the barbed wire for two weeks now and every day the butchering continues.

Like Datsun

Blessing Musariri

Amai Bettina's nagging desire to witness the evangelical miracles taking place in the sports stadium, gave rise to a most remarkable day. Not only was her wish unfulfilled, but events unfolded in a manner that left Amai Bettina – generally known for her outspokeness in the face of tribulation – forever suspended in a state of wonder.

Had she been capable of speech on reaching her small bungalow in Unit G, Seke, when asked by her ever-solemn child how her day had been, Amai Bettina would have responded with gusto, 'Bettina *mwana'ngu!* What I saw today?' A shake of the head, palms clapped together, 'You would not like it. Never in your life!' And, this prelude over, she would begin her story from the most logical place – the beginning.

'Do you remember Bettina, the year your father's relatives came here to pay reparations for all the wrongs your father inflicted upon me?'

Bettina did remember because what had followed was a confusing period in which her mother had suffered an unmanageable surplus of funds. Amai Bettina, never having had so much money before, had not known what to do with it. She did not have a bank account – she did not know anyone who did – but her real problem was that if the money were to serve its purpose, it should be spent on herself and her relatives,

45

but not on her children, who were considered as one with their father. The trouble was that Amai Bettina had long fallen out with her relatives and was not prepared to entertain any ideas, which they might have had, about sharing her fortune – though whether it was good fortune, was increasingly questionable. So, despite Bettina's need for new uniforms and textbooks, Amai Bettina was eventually forced into giving generous bequests to those relatives whose offences she re-evaluated as pardonable.

'Amongst many of the misdemeanours of your father – the only person ever, to see the end of my patience, is the issue of Datsun 120Y.'

Inexplicably, Amai Bettina always referred to the rusty yellow heap of metal on wheels as if she was talking about a person – naDatsun 120Y *uyu*, she would say, instead of neDatsun 120Y *iyo* – a thing. Everyone simply adjusted, as they did to all Amai Bettina's peculiarities, she was simply that kind of person.

'Anyway, your father left the house saying he was going to the store to buy jam. Did I tell you this story before, Bettina? No I don't think so.' She had. Many times, but Bettina knowing better would hold her silence. 'Anyway, he came back, naDatsun 120Y *uyu*. That by itself was not a crime. Ayewha! No, there's no crime when a hard-working person uses his money to improve his life. But your father wouldn't have known hard work if it crept into his trousers and said a nice hullo. No! So he stood there, proudly showing me Datsun, and telling me that he'd found a good use for the money *I'd* been saving – *my* money, from *my* groundnut harvest. Mine. From which, amongst other things, I was going to buy blankets for *my* mothers.'

On that day, after chewing off her husband's ear with cutting precision and a mild attack of the dramatics – rolling around on the ground and wailing to the neighbourhood at large about the misappropriation of her funds – Amai Bettina rallied and roundly declared, 'Datsun *uyu ka*, is going to be the death of me.' It was said with such conviction, it was almost a promise.

And, had she been capable of speech on her return from her outing, she would have said, 'Bettina, *mwanangu*, I never spoke a truer word that day! Now, you saw me get up this morning, like I do every day, *ka? Eh-*

be-e. So I said to myself, 'Amai Bettina, today is the day that you will go to this new church and see for yourself, gold and diamonds falling from the sky to cover the congregation. You can hear only so much from other people before you have to see with your own eyes. Didn't you tell me Bettina that you heard about women's skirts falling off their bodies because the pastor had performed a weight-loss miracle? What about those bald heads that grew hair right there and then? I was finally going to see such things for myself. Han'ti, they say, to see is to believe?

So, even though I've cursed your father all these years that he's been gone, buying Datsun made me learn how to drive – I was not about to let him show off in a car bought by my sweat. For this only I am grateful, because if I'd asked your *'mainini* Selma to come with me, she would have reported me to Pastor Mapatya, and you wouldn't have liked the talk that resulted. But, see now, you would never believe it, for all these years, Datsun has not given me a problem, even though, to look at him, you would think that he's going nowhere. I never thought he would last so long, but he has. In fact, if Datsun could have paid *roora* and given me children I would've gladly taken him as my husband. Nevertheless, I said it, didn't I? Datsun *uyu ka*, is going to be the death of me, and if you can believe it, today is the day that Datsun died for me in the middle of the road. *Mwana'ngu!* Again, the shaking head the thrown out palms – this time, a surrender.

So, there Amai Bettina was – too far from home to walk back, too far from her destination to walk forward. In any case, Amai Bettina was not interested in going back, only forwards. Because Datsun had served her so well over the years, her first instinct was to investigate the trouble without any feelings of rancour; she was almost certain that it could not be anything too debilitating. Surely Datsun would rally, it was just one of those setbacks that afflicted him from time to time. And, as luck would have it, she'd been within sight of a service station.

'Haaa moms...' the young man in the greasy overalls was shaking his head, as he withdrew from under the hood, '...this is a *real* break-down. How've you been driving this car all this time? Let me just tell you that it's seen its last kilometre today. I can't even begin to tell you about the rust in your engine.' Again, he shook his head. Amai Bettina felt a rising irritation. What did he know about Datsun? He didn't deserve the dollar she had discreetly slipped from her handbag, ready to give him when he'd fixed the problem. She slipped it back into her bag as the young man wiped his hands with the rag from the back of his overalls' pocket. So this is how it was to be: even Datsun disapproved of her desire to attend a church so outside her faith that he'd chosen to die rather than take her there. He was just as censorious as her younger sister Selma, who said it once and said it again, 'Sisi, remember 1 John 4 vs 1 and heed it well. "Beware of false prophets".'

Even though she didn't want to believe it, Amai Bettina was not one to say that it was night when she could see for herself that the sun was shining. In truth, Datsun had long outlived her expectations. Even though momentarily she'd been angry with him, as she'd been angry with her husband at the time of his death, she was inclined to forgive him this one complete let-down, especially considering it was the first of such magnitude and likely to be the last.

Amai Bettina was thankful for the convenience of living in the townships, the streets were never deserted, even at 8.30 on a Sunday morning. So there'd been enough hands to help her park Datsun off the road. She could see that being on the dusty shoulder would cause an obstruction for other vehicles, which would need to veer off the patchy tarmac to avoid the crater-sized potholes, but she felt she could live with such a burden on her conscience. So she hoisted her heavy black vinyl handbag over her shoulder and set off in the direction of her sister's house, with the intention of begging a ride into town. She knew that they would still be at home, as they had all attended church the day before.

'If you can imagine, Bettina!' And she would have leant forward in her seat, the one where she always sat, no matter who was visiting as if a homing device had been implanted in her firm, rounded bottom, one that unerringly guided her to a sofa that now bore the imprint of her buttocks and would no longer acquiesce to the presence of any other behind but hers. 'That, one moment I'm walking down the street, thanking my Lord that I still have good use of two healthy legs, when I'm lifted from the ground, my ears are assaulted by a sound so loud that it left only a ringing in my head. And then, Bettina, a hand, a real human hand, flies out of the air and slaps me in the face as I land in someone's vegetable garden.' Her own hands would have been flapping in fervent demonstration of the whole event. Bettina, used to her mother's theatrics, would have waited patiently to hear the whole story before sharing what she'd recently heard on local TV during the afternoon news.

It was the most shocking thing indeed, and it had taken place at a house several feet from where Selma resided. Amai Bettina was at least five minutes away when the explosion happened, reducing one house to rubble and damaging several others in the vicinity, and heralded, 'The Mystery Blast that Rocked Chitungwiza'. But for all Amai Bettina knew, lying winded, on top of someone's patch of chomolia with a body-less appendage, now obscenely nestled in her bosom, it could only be explained as a supernatural event of notable proportions.

Thoroughly bewildered, Amai Bettina was unable to process the horror of the scene; not even to shriek and recoil from the charred flesh that had unceremoniously placed itself in her custody. Eyes wide open, mouth agape in wordless amazement, Amai Bettina sat up, shifting the bloody hand as if distractedly removing the roving hand of a toddler from her breast, and forgot to let it go as she heaved herself to her feet. Her bag lay trampled in the street, unnoticed by the crowd that surged forth from their houses, heading towards the scene of the explosion. Her 1950s bouffant wig, lay ruined in the indentation her body had made amidst the stalks and leaves where she had landed.

While the whole neighbourhood gravitated to what was later to be described as a grisly scene of destruction, Amai Bettina, trapped in the unseeing, unhearing world of those whose spirits have received too unexpected a fright, drifted to a deserted street market set up underneath a mango tree and sat on the upturned wooden crate that served as a stool. It was there among the bright tomatoes, mangoes, *maputi*, open packets of singly wrapped sweets and chewing gum, that a police detail found her. By this time, a small group of children stood silently watching her, curious about the macabre appendage that dangled from her grasp. Wide-eyed, they simply stared, unsure of whether or not to be frightened. Quite literally, the entire neighbourhood had temporarily migrated to the site of the disaster and were still milling about, waiting to receive an explanation as to what had taken place. The most disturbing theories were being proffered – surely medicine such as this should be left safely across the borders from whence it came.

At this point in recounting the story of her day to Bettina, Amai Bettina might have finally reclined in her seat, exhausted at last and said, 'Ah Bettina, I was finished. This is what comes of being curious about strange miracles. Truly it is the last hour.' Her hands would fall into her lap and remain there, awaiting their next cue. Then, 'Imagine what I must have looked like. The policemen who found me had been dispatched to measure the extent of the blast – they were following the trail of shrapnel and body parts. I couldn't tell you how they moved me from where I sat, or how Selma and her husband spotted me. All these things, I could not say because when I fell ... or was I thrown back? I cannot clearly recall, but when I landed, I fell so hard that I must have dislodged my soul and even now, it has not yet recovered its rightful place within me.'

Bettina, hearing the entirety of her mother's strange and gruesome tale, would want to tell her then, not of miracles, but of powerful magic gone horribly wrong. She would have wanted to tell her mother that stories abounding were those of a renowned traditional healer who had called a conference of other healers, and along with his client, tried to behead a money-making goblin obtained from a powerful sangoma across the border. The magic of the fetish being too advanced for them, the spell had gone wrong and caused an almighty explosion that ripped those present into pieces, completely destroyed the house and damaged several others, mysteriously leaving only the traditional healer's clay pot untouched, right at the epicentre of the blast. She would want to say, 'Mama you were not the only one pelted by flying bits of flesh, it was everywhere, landing in people's homes and gardens, but what a terrible thing to have happened to you.'

But Bettina would not get the chance to tell her mother any of this. Seeing her mother stagger in towards the end of day supported by her Amainini Selma and her husband, Bettina immediately discerned that, of all her mother's dramatic moments, this was not one of the usual laughable variety. She did not like the absent look in her mother's eyes, the sluggishness of her movements and the strain around her mouth. When she asked with alarm, what the matter was, she was met by a shaking of the head by both her aunt and uncle, as they took her mother past her, to lay her down gently on the bed in her room. Heart bumping crazily in her chest, Bettina asked the thing that allowed her to avoid hearing the worst of what might be coming: 'Where is Datsun? Did Amai have an accident? What happened? Amainini please tell me.'

Amainini Selma related to Bettina what she had managed to piece together after talking to people in the neighbourhood. For her part, the first she knew of the disturbance was when a brick had come flying through the window of her house, four doors down from the blast. Thankfully, no one had been hurt. Once the dust settled a little, Selma and her husband had cautiously ventured out to investigate. After what had seemed like hours, moving around the crowd at the scene and collecting scattered information – mainly conjecture, from bystanders – Selma had happened to catch sight of her sister being ushered by police to a vehicle that was taking injured people to the hospital, and claimed her. Her husband had walked back in Amai Bettina's footsteps up to the point where he came across Datsun, abandoned by the side of the road, causing even more of an obstruction as peak hour for traffic was inching towards its climax.

'It's over for that car,' he said, 'it was more than a break-down, that car is now dead. It's a wonder it survived this long.'

When Bettina finally asked the question she'd been dreading, she was informed that the wait at the hospital had been so terribly long that Amai Bettina, not having said a word since they found her, had begun to agitate vociferously to be taken home. Selma and her husband had tried to calm her down and insist she stay and be looked at by a doctor, but Amai Bettina's agitation had threatened to become the new danger to her well-being and so they had capitulated and brought her home. She had been subdued ever since.

'We will stay here with you, Bettina, in case she comes round or needs some assistance. Why don't you go and put some water on to boil for a cup of tea. Han'ti, a cup of sweet tea is good for shock?' Selma wringing her hands, sought comfort in whatever small wisdom she could recall. Failing access to anything more than that, she settled on her default position, 'Let us pray. We are in darkness right now, these are bad times, bad people among us, bad medicine. 1 John 2 v18, "Little children, it is the last hour ..."' She petered off as she sank into the unyielding sofa, which even now, seemed to make a point of being as uncomfortable as possible for any other than Amai Bettina. Across from her, her husband stretched out his long legs and crossed his thin ankles and heaved a loud sigh, announcing the start of a long vigil.

And so it happened, that after several prayers and muted conversation, Bettina, Amainini Selma and her husband subsided, one by one, into sleep. Meanwhile, in the next room, Amai Bettina, whose fragile heart had survived all her melodramas thus far, beat steadily several hours into the sleep-filled night, and just as morning gave birth to its first light, gave a light fluttering, an unuttered cough and just like Datsun, stuttered into everlasting silence.

Trespassers

Chiedza Musengezi

Chembe lies on his bed, floating between wakefulness and sleep. It is May. The chill of an approaching winter stirs him awake. He slides under the blankets and stretches out an arm to put out a candle, crushing the burning wick between thumb and forefinger. A smell of candle fumes lingers. He fluffs up a pillow, positions it, but before he lays his head down, there is a confident rap at the door. It is nine o'clock in the evening. Outside a full moon rises.

'Who is it?'

'It's me.'

It is Jailos. Chembe can tell from the timbre of the voice. Jailos assists with security duties on Chapisa Farm. He's on duty tonight. Chembe waits to hear what the matter is.

'Two men want to talk to you. They want to see only foreman.'

Chembe reaches for his overalls that hang on a chair beside the bed. He wears his boots, pulls a woollen hat over his head and picks up a baton and torch from a corner. The two men stride along a path one behind the other. Jailos leads the way at a fast pace. Chembe thinks the young man is either afraid or excited.

'Who are these people?'

'Don't know. They won't speak to me.'

It is a clear night with a star-studded sky. Definitive shapes of farm buildings are visible; the farm school, tobacco barns, empty horse stables, garage and tool sheds. The torch beam sometimes falls on the thatch of a cooking hut or on the asbestos sheet of a farmhand's main house as they go past the farm compound. They head towards a locked gate. Two figures stand near the stile as if ready to climb over the fence. One is tall, the other of medium height. The rosette of light turns this way and that before Chembe focuses on the two strangers. A woollen scarf with brown stripes is wound round the neck of the taller one. The short man wears a beret at an angle on his head. Both have their hands in their jacket pockets.

'Hey, switch off that thing. We're not thieves.' The taller one speaks.

Chembe tries to take the sting out of the stranger's words. 'Good evening, my brothers.' He directs the torch light to the ground. 'How can I help you?'

'You the foreman?"

Chembe nods his head.

'Just the man we're looking for. Eh, we want to come and address the workers some time. You arrange that for us, old man.' It is more a command than a question.

'Old man', Chembe heard the slight sneer of disrespect in these two English words. The old would not be part of this new order. Were not expected to either understand or appreciate it. Still, he politely informs them that he cannot allow strangers onto the farm. They have to seek permission from Mr Winterson, the farm owner. The young men have no interest in what he says. The short one has the last word before they melt into the bushes.

'These *vaenzi* will be back *chop chop.*'

Chembe realises perhaps he should not have used the word strangers, but that was the rule – no strangers without appointment – and the young men's attitude had not encouraged him to think they were men of good will.

Nonetheless, Jailos still complains, 'Mudhara Chembe, *hini nda-*

va? You talk like you're born out of the same womb. They could be thieves, troublemakers, vandalisers. We should have...' Jailos completes the sentence with a crossing of hands at the wrists mimicking a handcuffed person. Both Jailos and Chembe were issued with handcuffs after training with a security guard company in Harare.

'I know, but not so fast. They've not stolen or caused trouble. Better wait. See what they're up to first?'

'Up to no good,' insists Jailos.

Chembe thinks it's unwise to annoy strangers especially at night. They follow the fireguard that runs along the perimeter fence for about two hundred metres checking for loose strands where the barbed wire may have been cut. All is well. Jailos remains behind sitting by a fire in the small wooden shelter near the stile. Chembe returns to his house. He decides to pass by the farmhouse for a quick check. He strides through a windbreak of pine trees and up the slope of the hill where the house stands. He finds the security lights shining bright and the tall gate locked. Thwacks of electric current reassure him that the farmhouse perimeter fence is undisturbed.

One early morning, thirty-five years previously, Chembe arrived at Chapisa Farm. He had travelled forty kilometres from Harare by bus along the Mutoko Road then walked five kilometres along a dusty strip that branched off to the left of the main road. He waited at the farm's main gate among a group of people from the nearby Chikwaka Communal Lands looking for seasonal work. The farmer needed extra hands to help out with the tobacco crop. Experienced tobacco pickers and graders were selected. Chembe was not among them. However, he'd caught the attention of the white farmer and his assistant because of his seemingly underage appearance. A boy of medium height, slight of build, a hint of puppy fat underneath smooth face skin and upper arms without the firm bulge of hardened biceps.

'What farm experience do you have?' Mr Winterson stared down at the boy with his pale blue eyes.

'Me, I'm a grader. Fast grader of oranges at Mazowe Citrus Estate.' Chembe had been laid off at the estate because acreage under citrus plantation had been reduced to make way for maize growing.

'We grade tobacco here not oranges. What else did you do?'

'Me, I clean, wax and pack...o..oranges' his confidence crumbled.

'I see. You have only worked with oranges,' Feeling empathy for the youth, he thought that he was being illogical to expect work experience out of a boy who was still a child. 'How old are you?'

'Eighteen.'

It was a guess. His father, who originally came from Malawi, had left the citrus estate for the mines, where wages were said to be double what he was getting. He did not register the birth of either of his two children through ignorance or irresponsibility, who knows? When Chembe reached school-going age, he could not be enrolled in school without a certificate. His mother, who had never been to school, paid a man of Malawian origin to pose as the father at the Mazoe District Office. The hired father retained the first names of the children but gave them his surname. He stood before the clerk, presented the children along with his proof of identity. He plucked birthdays out of the air and the children acquired birth certificates and an identity, enabling Chembe to go to school, and later, to leave the citrus estate and seek a job elsewhere.

By ten o'clock that the morning it was warm. Chembe watched the farmer roll up the sleeves of his khaki shirt to his elbows exposing arms with veins that stood out like chords. He pulled at the wide brim of his hat to shield his eyes from the sun as he checked the identity documents of the job seekers. Recruitment of the temporary workers was close to complete, and Chembe still stood outside the gate. Mr Winterson was not an unkind man, and there was something about the youth's quiet persistence, which struck a chord with him. Impatience is not a virtue in a farmer.

Mr Winterson called for his assistant and instructed that the youth be employed in the vegetable section. Fifteen acres of Chipise Farm was under market gardening. Chembe would be watched for three months before being confirmed in the position.

The young man turned out to have the strength of an ox. He turned up early for work every day and was never absent without good reason. He sorted, cleaned and crated potatoes, tomatoes, butternut squash, cabbage, aubergines and cucumber. Always ready to help the new recruits Chembe impressed Mr Winterson with his social skills and eagerness to embrace new arrivals. He kept the young man at the back of his mind for when there was a more responsible post to be filled.

Chembe shared a two-roomed house in the farm compound with another young farmhand. In five years he grew taller and his body filled out. He sported a beard on his chin. Well liked by the rest of the farmhands, some mothers expressed the view that he would make an ideal son-in-law.

So it was that Chembe met Snodia, a seasonal worker from Chikwaka Communal Lands, which border the eastern side of Chapisa Farm. He liked her dark complexion and her big eyes set in a round open face that made her seem as if she had no secrets. Once she accepted his proposal for marriage, Chembe did not waste time. He wanted to be introduced to her family immediately but the visit to Snodia's parents was a not great success.

Chembe spoke Shona fluently but with the inflections of Chichewa, his mother tongue. Snodia and her boyfriend were sitting in the grandmother's hut with members of her family who had come to meet their son-in-law-to-be. They found, or pretended to find, his speech hard to understand.

'Huh? What did you say?' Snodia's aunt, mother, grandmother or uncle would ask when Chembe spoke. Sometimes Snodia would intervene to clarify a point or provide an appropriate word or its pronunciation. She was eager to make him blend in with the rest of the family. He masked his embarrassment with contrived cheerfulness and laughter. It was also an uncomfortable moment for Chembe who had to talk about his family history about which he had little knowledge.

'So where is your family? Snodia's aunt wanted to know.

Chembe talked about his mother and sister. The mother had died and his young sister was a junior wife to an older man who had journeyed with his father from Malawi to what was then Rhodesia. He hardly had any recollection of his father who had left for Jumbo Mine when he was four years old. When his mother had followed his father to ask for money towards maintenance of the children, he was no longer there. Some of his friends said he had been seen on a ranch in Plumtree in the south west of Zimbabwe driving a herd of Brahmans to the feeding troughs. Chembe's mother gave up. She had neither money nor energy to chase after him.

'My father works in Matabeleland' was all Chembe could say.

At the end of the visit, when some relatives saw them out of the hut to the bus stop on the Harare-Mutoko Road, the grandmother tactlessly pulled Snodia aside.

'Throwing yourself away to a foreigner like that?' she whispered loudly. 'What's wrong with the local men? *Xnaa!* You're not wise.'

Snodia was taken aback by the old woman's outburst.

'It is better to settle down with someone you know, who has grown up with you. What is wrong with Togara, Misheck, Obey?' the old woman named the eligible young men in the village. 'And what do you know about the ways of your man's people?'

Snodia loved Chembe and she was going marry him, but she didn't want to upset her grandmother so she simply responded that he was a hard-working and honest man, much respected by the other farmworkers.

But her grandmother would not let up and carried on as if all Malawian people were one. '*MaBrandaya anotetereka.* They are drifters cursed with running away from their own people. They travel not to reach a destination.'

'Grandmother, you have never travelled further than Juru Growth Point,' she said pointing at an eclectic conglomeration of buildings in the distance, the communal lands' main contact with the outside world. 'How do you know about people who live in other parts?'

Snodia was upset; she rejoined the rest of the group. The grandmother turned and walked back at an uncharacteristic pace for one who walked with the aid of a walking stick. She too was upset that her wise counsel had not been well received by her own kith and kin.

Sharing her grandmother's concerns with Chembe strengthened his resolve to marry her. He approached Mr Winterson and told him about the imminent marriage. He hoped Mr Winterson might let him buy two old cows that he could put towards lobola. The cost would be deducted from his wages little by little. The farmer was not agreeable.

'I'll be setting an example. Opening floodgates. Before I blink every bloody farm worker would want a *mombe* from me. Out of the question.'

'But you're a father to me. I've grown up under your care. Most of what I can do on the farm you taught me.' Chembe knew Mr Winterson's bark was often much worse than his bite, and he was was quietly conscious that he had successfully replaced the blue gums with indigenous trees; he could plough the fields, cure and grade tobacco as well as grow all the vegetables from seed. 'Who else would help me build my family?'

And Chembe was right. Mr Winterson had three grown sons who had immigrated to South Africa, and not much outlet for his paternal instincts. So, on reflection, Mr Winterson agreed to help, but only if his wife concurred.

'Give the young chap a chance. You always talk about what a good worker he is.' Mrs Winterson did not often go down to the fields but she knew Chembe from the clinic she ran on the farm and from the many times he brought vegetables to the farmhouse. She knew her husband felt affection for the young man founded on mutual trust, his work ethic and his admirable character. He would like Chembe to be happy, with a family of his own. He felt he deserved a chance at life.

Once Chembe had paid *lobola*, his standing with his in-laws improved. Of the three young men who had married into the family he was the only one who had paid off the bride's wealth. Being a farm hand the in-laws found him helpful around the homestead. He was especially attentive to the grandmother who had finally warmed to him. She had a ready list of chores for him when he visited: logs to be chopped for firewood, a broken garden fence to be mended or door to be put back on its hinges. And Snodia's grandmother knew how to show her appreciation. Chembe often walked out of her yard on a full stomach, a fat pullet under his arm, a gift for his family at the farm. Sometimes he would bring saplings of *musasa*, *mubvee*, duikerberry and other local trees he was planting on the farm, to the pleasure of his father-in-law.

The years passed generally peacefully and productively, and the couple had two children, Madalitso and Mayamiko. When they reached school age, the pressure from Snodia's family for Chembe to build a house in Chikwakwa began to make more sense, especially as it meant that the children could go to the local Anglican mission school that had qualified teachers. The pre-school on the farm had been good, Snodia had participated, and taken a course run by Save the Children, but the primary school still depended on O-level school leavers.

And so it was that over several years, with small loans here, and hard work there, Snodia and Chembe built a brick house in Chikwaka with five rooms and a corrugated iron roof. The woman had begun to live there with the childen long before the final nail was struck. And while Chembe missed them, his work on the farm as foreman kept him fully occupied from dawn to dusk and he always joined the family at weekends, cycling fifteen kilometers each Friday on a bicycle laden with packets of potatoes, onions and tomatoes. And sometimes she and the children would return to the farm, especially during the school holidays, when Maladitso, loved to ride the tractors, everyone turning a blind eye, given Chembe's position.

But all good things come to an end, Maladitso returned one day from school with his clothes dirty, and covered in cuts and bruises. 'Whatever have you done?' his mother asked, hastily filling a bowl of cold water. 'Hondo called my father a foreigner, a white man's lap dog. He said that soon he would be out of a job, and that his own father would have land on Chapisa Farm. He said Mr Winterston is a thief and must go back to England.'

Snodia felt the struggle, which had been on the lips of every market woman for weeks now, coming right into their home. She took a wet cloth and bathed the cut on Maladitso's forehead, as if he were a small child, and not a young man. She wondered what she should say to him. She knew people were jealous of she and Chembe because of the loans they had been given by Mr Winterston, because of all the free vegetables and firewood. But hadn't her husband worked for it over almost two decades now; didn't he deserve the respect of his employer? But she knew too that when the chips were down, the fact that he'd been born in Zimbabwe would count for nothing. People would turn on him, and call him a traitor, a Malawian dog. Should her son receive the same treatment?

Maladitso looked at her. 'ZBC says we should go and take the farms, drive out the white man. Do we not need land? I fought Hondo because he insulted my father, but I am not defending the farm.'

Snodia felt that she should go and see Chembe; the only way was to talk to him. Her heart was filled with misgiving. But he should be back home in two days – that is if he came on Friday, as usual. She decided that it would be best to wait, and that if he did not come, she would go to the farm on Sunday.

On Friday Chembe had been unusually late to arrive, Snodia had been out twice to the bus stop, looking for him. Her anxiety built with the noise of the dogs barking, a familiar sound but one that grated against chafed nerves. Then someone with a familiar scent stepped into the yard. '*Fusek! Choka,*' she heard Chembe mutter, shooing away their two dogs. Once he'd settled, Snodia served him sadza and dried mushrooms in peanut butter. Afterwards she heated up bath water for her husband who was washing down his dinner with heavily sugared black tea from his favourite tin mug. He disliked china cups that he said were so small they could not hold a mouthful.

They were in bed when Snodia brought up the subject of trouble on the farms.

'If I were you I would leave the job,' Snodia's voice was low.

'Why? And do what? Watch my family go hungry?'

'It's not your farm. Keep out of it.'

'Keep out of what?'

'You told me there are strangers about?'

'Ah, nothing new. People wander from the reserves to cut thatch grass, collect firewood… Winterson doesn't mind, so long as they ask.'

'They don't ask these days. They say it's their land. Haven't they already invaded the neighbourhood farms – Norfolk, Serui, Nyabira … You *must* know this?' Snodia's firm voice trailed away. 'Don't chase

61

them, setting dogs after them like you do. You'll only invite trouble for the family.'

Snodia did not reveal that their son had aleady had a fight with a group of youths who had come under the influence of the local councillor. How long would it be before he joined them. He was at that very impressionable age. Her best friend had told her that she could do nothing with her own son who was being paid to join the invaders, and he's given *mbanje*, the woman said helplessly. 'Nothing can I do, not when he's been smoking and drinking – and we need the money.' Snodia felt she knew better than her husband how these invasions were going to break up families, break up communities. When something was free, everyone would want a share of it.

'You're living in a cocoon,' she told him. Here in Chiwaka everyone is talking about these invasions. 'People are divided, but they all want land.'

'Yes, but they want food, jobs, firewood too,' said Chembe refusing to hear the anxiety in her voice. There'd been troubles before. They would pass.

'Winterson is not a politics man, only a farmer.' Chembe laughed the way he did when he thought an idea was far-fetched, though deep in his heart he worried too

Back on the farm Mr Winterson asked Chembe to increase the patrols. There was an upsurge of people who wandered across the lands without permission. Chembe, as foreman, was asked to double up as head of security. He found a way to cut down on moving up, down and across the farm. He climbed the *musamvi* tree that grew on a rise of the fifty acres of local trees. It was a big, tall tree with great limbs; its leafy boughs formed a wide thick canopy. Where the trunk divided one branch grew up and outwards then curved on itself into the shape of the letter L. Chembe followed the branch and sat in the bend, his legs resting on the smaller branches beneath. With his head partially hidden in the foliage he would sit quietly and people could walk past underneath without noticing him. Climbing trees was a childhood habit. His position gave him an excellent observation point. From this height, Chapisa Farm spread out like a map beneath him. He could see red of the farmhouse roof, the dam that shone like a sheet of glass to the south of the vlei and the dairy herd grazing. Besides being a look out, it gave Chembe real pleasure. He enjoyed the solitude of the woods: the breeze stirring the leaves, twigs, leaves, cracking pods, and the many birds that came to feast on *tsampi* fruit, the pea-sized sweet figs, which he also sometimes ate.

Chembe was in the *musamvi* tree when two men walked past beneath him. He recognised the tall man with the striped woollen scarf. The strangers were back. Chembe quickly and quietly climbed down the tree and followed them at a distance. He saw them talking to Jailos, who was watching over the women from Chikwaka whom Chembe had granted permission to cut thatch grass. He strained to catch snippets of the conversation. The tall one seemed to raise his voice deliberately as if he knew he was being followed, and as if he wanted to be sure that Chembe heard his every word. This being the case, Chembe strolled up to them, and nodded.

'The white farmer is going to leave,' the stranger continued with barely a glance in Chembe's direction. 'He has already had our letter. It's now twenty-one years since the country got its independence. He has made enough money. Now, it's our turn. We are going to parcel out the farm in ten, twenty, thirty and fifty acres for people to farm. Jailos glances at Chembe with eyes that say the idea is sound.

'I would say a man who owns land is a free man Mudhara Chembe. You grow your own food. Feed your family. You go to the fields in your own time. Nobody shouts at you.'

The strangers smile, nodding in agreement. Chembe reflects. It is all very well for a young man like Jailos to talk like this. He has no family. What would stop a young man from trying a new life? His position is different. He has a family. Mr Winterson has been good to him. It would be better for him to live with the difficulties that he knows. What other hazards might lie ahead? Has Jailos been seeing these men secretly? It's a discomforting thought.

'Experienced farmers like you, we give thirty acres of good land.' The tall one points at the ploughed fields. We will give you a plough, two oxen and maize seed. What more can you ask?'

'But who are you? You have no permission to be here. Now you talk about taking over the farm. I have to tell Winterson.'

'You'll soon know. But go ahead and call him.'

Chembe hurries towards the farmhouse. A plume of smoke rising where the women are cutting grass halts him. He changes direction, trots towards them. He is angry that the grass-cutters are acting against the rules, starting a fire that can easily spread. Chembe confronts them but the women are unperturbed. They have to eat and they need to cook because they will be cutting grass for the next three days. Chembe is taken aback.

'I'm going to call Winterson. He has to see for himself.'

The women laugh and jeer. 'What can your white man do?' says one.

It's clear that what has been happening in the neighbourhood has finally arrived at Chipise.

Chembe hears a crowd in the distance. It's shouting and singing. *'Jambanja jambanja,'* and is armed with machetes, knobkerries and bicycle chains. One holds aloft the signpost that has been uprooted from the farm entrance. The inscription reads 'Chapisa Farm. Trespassers will be prosecuted.' It heads towards the forest of indigenous trees close to where the grass cutters are. The women put down their sickles and join the crowd ululating and dancing. Chembe winces at the thuds of axes felling trees that he has tended for years.

One of the workers alerts the farmer who phones the police. He drives twenty kilometres to Goromonzi Police Station to pick up the officers because they have no vehicle. He brings back three officers. The senior one sits in the front with his hat on. He has a baton in his lap and drums on it with his thumb. The younger officers share the back seat, which smells of dog fur. There is silence in the car. The Land Rover swerves as the farmer hastily takes corners on the strip road. The senior officer instructs the farmer not to rush.

When they arrive the farm workers have gathered to watch what is happening. The tall man encourages them to join in. Chembe spots Mayamiko in the crowd. Their eyes meet. The son looks down, averting his father's gaze. He looks rough and smells rougher. His eyes are red and tired. His hair is uncombed and his clothes have the sickly tang of old sweat. Chembe is shocked, embarrassed, angry and sorry for his son all at once.

The police officers do not restrain the crowd. The senior officer turns to the white farmer. 'This is outside our control. You have to talk to each other and reach a compromise. The farm belongs to all of you. These are their ancestral lands too.'

'I will not.' The farmer is now red in the face. He turns to the farm workers. They look passive and cowed. He clears his throat. He shuts his eyes as if to make everything disappear. There is a silence. Heads drop. The workers look at each other's face covertly. The farmer's inner ear replays the police officer's words: 'This is outside... ancestral lands.'

Tension makes the white farmer's words tumble out through a half-open mouth. 'The land grabbers are here... you're welcome to join them ... if you wish.' Anger shakes his voice and halts his speech. 'If you think they've come for land... I'm afraid you're mistaken. They're thieves, sniffing round my property like a pack of wild dogs. They're after my dairy herd, my cured tobacco, my farm equipment... You can go with them...Go on!'

Muffled sniggers came from the invading crowd followed by a wave of shock that ripples through the gathering of farm workers. A shuffle of feet draws his attention. Jailos and a small group of farmhands saunter away towards the group that has come to the farm.

'We're for land,' Jailos's speech is loud, slow and deliberate.

The farmer interrupts the cheers and whistles, a show of support by the incomers for the farmhands that have joined them.

'Good riddance to all of you, if you go. Do you think those people care about you? You'll be on your own. And God help you because I won't. No more free school for your children. No more free rations of maize meal, beans... No more free clinic when you're sick. And in a few years, when all the trees are cut down, this land will be barren.' He points at the acacia tree-clothed anthills beyond the ploughed wheat fields, the designated burial ground for farm workers. 'No more decent burials when the time comes. ... ' He pauses.

65

In the silence a few of the farm workers turn their eyes to the anthills where remains of their relatives lie beneath mounds of earth with up-turned battered ceremonial dishes on the top and planted crude wooden crosses bearing the name of a baby, mother, brother or grandparent in the spidery scrawl of those who have not gone beyond the second grade of primary school. He too looks at a clump of white flowering bougainvilleas that cover up the graves of three generations of the Wintersons. Tears unexpectedly well in the farmer's eyes. He chokes with emotion. Not just years, but a century of work and investment. Chembe moves close to him. The police officers glare at the farm workers who murmur protest.

'We can call for riot police,' the senior officer hushes the farm workers.

'You have twenty-four hours to leave the farm. Out! *NomuBrantyre wako*. Foreigners!' the tall man shouts. 'And that includes you, Chembe. You're a Malawian, a white man's poodle. Get out. Go! We're better off without you!'

Mbuya, My Grandmother

Sekai Nzenza

At dawn the rooster from our village compound makes the first call, others from nearby villages and across the river follow in full throat. Then a peaceful and almost serene silence falls on the soft air.

I leave the village compound long before sunrise every day. I walk down the valley, then climb the kopje to the high granite rocks and listen to the morning. My grandmother Mbuya VaMandirowesa is buried here on the flat part of the rocks where my mother laid out her crops to dry during the harvest season. VaMandirowesa was the first of my grandfather Sekuru Dhikisoni's five wives. We called her Mbuya Va-Mandirowesa, or just Mbuya.

She has been dead for twenty years now.

Every morning, I come here to wait for the sunrise over Simukai Mountains. I sit, think and dream. Flashbacks. The past and the present come together. Memories of the village. Visions and images merging, dissolving and blurring. At times, the past is so vivid, I hear the voice of Mbuya VaMandirowesa – laughing, talking, shouting, singing. I hear her. And I remember our lives back then, long before independence came, and we, the young ones, moved to the cities.

It is the beginning of October, the end of the dry season. The smell of last night's veld fires permeates the air. Smoke from the scattered village huts below shoots up to the sky. Then it spreads out, like a thin cloud, to merge with the mist from the valley. I sit waiting to see the sun rise over the mountains. The morning birds greet each other and there is the odd distant rooster's crow – cockarookoo. I hear baboons fighting high up in the Mbire Mountains further down the Save River. I listen to the wind. It comes from the valley below and blows over the granite rocks. The big trees that used to shield this place from it are long gone. When Mbuya, Sekuru Dhikisoni and the rest of the extended family were settled here by the Southern Rhodesia government in the 1930s, this was virgin land. Lions, giraffes, elephants, buffaloes, wildebeests, elands, kudus, impalas and rhinos roamed these mountains and valleys. Sekuru Dhikisoni and his brothers used to hunt and shoot elands, wild pigs and bucks up in the Hwedza mountains and in the Save river basin. Those big animals are gone now. Some were hunted and eaten as game meat. The rest were rounded up and taken to the game parks. All that is left in these hills are baboons, rabbits, snakes, birds, squirrels, skunks and all kinds of butterflies and insects.

People still slash and burn in the dry season. There are burnt axe-mutilated tree trunks everywhere: black soot and white ash blowing in the cold, early morning wind. The spring rains in September yeilded nothing but a little shower, leaving the burnt grass thirsting for more. Except for a few water holes, our two nearest rivers, Chidzikisa and Chinyika, are dry. We drink from the same spot – people, cattle, goats, and the baboons.

From these high granite rocks, I have 360-degree views of the valley below and the surrounding mountains. When I was growing up, the land below the granite kopje and near the river was very productive. There was plenty to eat. The hills were full of wild fruits – a fruit for every season. But now the land is tired and produces little. I can also see our village compound from here. Although many people have left for the city and the former white-owned farms, it is still a huge old compound with several huts and granaries. It was built long before I was born in the foothills of the Simukai mountains. A few kilometres behind the mountains lies the Save River. It winds smoothly like a big snake all the way to the Limpopo River bordering Zimbabwe and South Africa and then it pours its waters into the Indian Ocean.

Long before I left this village, I used to sleep on the mat next to the fire with Mbuya in her kitchen hut, the hut in which I was born. In those days, Mbuya used to rule the village. A tall, formidable woman, she walked with her hands clasped behind her back. She had a roundish face and a small medium flat nose; her dark chocolate brown skin was very smooth. On each of her cheekbones were two black tattoo marks, *nyora*, the traditional marks of beauty. Her whole stomach was covered with various patterns of beautiful *nyora*. When I touched them while we slept, I felt the bumps made by the *nyora* keloid scars. Mbuya told us that in her youthful days, a girl without *nyora* was not considered beautiful. After her first monthly period, every girl was given the intricate *nyora* patterns on her stomach. If she was brave enough, she had some done on her breasts as well. Mbuya visited the woman tattooist three times before she got married. She had many cuts made with a razor. They bled and the tattooist rubbed crushed black charcoal paste into each bleeding incision to stop infection and to give the *nyora* line its black colour. Mbuya gave the tattooist a basket of ground millet as a token of gratitude. She said it gave men pleasure to look at the *nyora* and feel the uneven stomach. Apart from the *nyora*, a woman wore rolls of waistline beads, playthings for the man in bed. When she stopped meeting Sekuru *pabonde*, Mbuya hid her beads in the granary. She told me that I would inherit the beads on the day I leave for my future husband's village.

Mbuya did not wear a doek to cover her head like all the married women in the village compound. Her hair was completely white and she cut it very short or shaved it. She wore small copper earrings, several copper bracelets, black rubber bands and brass rings around her ankles. She also often wore a black quilt thrown diagonally across her long brown dress tied at the top of one shoulder. Imposing and barefoot, she walked around the village compound, inspecting and examining everything with her eagle eyes.

Mbuya VaMandirowesa was feared by many people in this village. Not even her husband Sekuru VaDhikisoni and the other village elders could tell her what to do. My mother and the rest of the *varoora* kept away from her in case her sharp tongue lashed out at them for some wrong-doing.

She had stopped sharing the sleeping mat, *pabonde*, with Sekuru Dhikisoni. She said she was past the age of sex. Sekuru did not argue with her: he spent the nightly rotations among his four younger wives. But Mbuya was not that old. I often saw her run faster than many women when chasing baboons from the maize field or running away from the rain. Nobody could beat her on the dance floor either during an all-night *bira* or the *kurova guva* – ceremonies to honour our ancestral spirits.

Mbuya wanted me to sleep with her because she needed company at night. Only at night. During the day, she spent the whole afternoon with her sister-in-law and best friend, VaMakumbi. The whole village knew that Mbuya VaMandirowesa and VaMakumbi were inseparable. VaMakumbi was at least ten years younger than Mbuya. All day they sat under the *mutondo* tree behind Mbuya's hut talking, taking snuff and drinking village beer. Up to the time I was four, I played on their laps and they told me stories. They taught me how to count in Shona through song and dance – the way they used to count before white men brought numbers to Africa. The counting song went like this:

Motsiro	*Pamuromo*
Dendere	*Pegange*
Ragara	*Gangiridza*
Mashangwe	*Marindohwe*
Mbirimbizha	*Gumi rawa!*

When we reached ten, they let me clap my hands together and shout *'gumi rawa!'* and dance for them. I learnt to count to ten that way. Mbuya and VaMakumbi always laughed a great deal. They chased me away from sitting with them when I was old enough to repeat their conversations word for word. Sometimes I sneaked behind the granary near the *mutondo* tree and heard everything. They often gossiped about other people's sex lives. I understood nothing when they spoke in *tsumo nemadimikira*, riddles and metaphors. Sometimes when I brought them pieces of roast meat and salted peanuts, I saw tears of laughter in their eyes. If they were really happy VaMakumbi played the *mbira* and they sang the songs of their youth. VaMakumbi was the village tsuri, the singer well known for her beautiful singing voice. Mbuya played the rattle, *hosho*. They danced, sang and laughed. They also sang and played the *mbira* and *hosho* and danced when they were really sad as well, which was not that often. After sunset Mbuya accompanied VaMakumbi to her hut three compounds away. On the way, they stopped and talked, stopped and talked until they reached the entrance of VaMakumbi's hut. Then they came back together again, talking, laughing and even singing until they arrived at Mbuya's hut entrance. Then they went back again. They went back and forth like this three or four times until they settled in one hut and ate sadza together. Usually the sadza with dried meat in peanut sauce that I would have cooked for them. After one or two songs, they danced without any co-ordination. The following afternoon they would be under the *mutondo* tree again doing what they did yesterday, as almost every day during the dry season. Moonlight or no moonlight. Except on days when the two of them came down to the river to bathe with the women and girls. Then they would be with us all afternoon, only to meet up again after sunset and start drinking and taking snuff. An afternoon spent bathing and scrubbing their feet at the river made them tired. So, they often retired to their huts early. VaMakumbi still had a husband waiting for her. She was the only wife with no junior wives behind her.

When my Mbuya came down to the river to bathe with the women, she brought her one old dress, a black petticoat, a black quilt and some other rags. *Varoora*, the women who married into our large extended family, fought over who should wash her dirty clothes. They all wanted to please Mbuya and gain her favour.

Down at the river Mbuya was a different person. She was relaxed, warm and not authoritative. I scrubbed and massaged her back with a stone while Piri did the same to VaMakumbi. Piri was my cousin, my father's brother's daughter. When Mbuya was all scrubbed and clean, she put peanut oil all over her body, proud of her *nyora* there for all to see and admire. All the married women at the river wore colourful beads

71

around their waists for beauty. This added to their sexual allure. Mbuya no longer wore any beads. All her beads were safely stored away. Instead of waist beads, she wore a piece of old string with a little seed from a medicinal tree. This seed used to stop her from getting pregnant. Now it stopped her from getting backache and painful joints.

Mbuya and VaMakumbi inspected the number of bead rows on the women's waists. They meticulously examined the type and colour of the beads. The larger the number of rows sitting on a big covetous bottom, the more beautiful and fertile the woman. The women paraded themselves naked and endlessly laughed and teased each other about the size of their bottoms and legs. Mbuya said that a new *muroora* without a variety of waist beads could not be good *pabonde*. This woman was therefore not cultured enough to have married into our family. Soon after marriage, a young woman must get pregnant. If she took more than a year to do so, Mbuya and VaMakumbi took her aside and questioned her art of love-making. They counted the number of beads she carried.

We, young girls, did not wear any beads. We were still the village virgins, waiting for the right time to learn the mysteries of sex and motherhood. I wanted to become a full woman, so I could inherit Mbuya's beads. One day those colourful beads, passed on from my great grandmother, will grace *chiuno changu*, my waist. They will warm the loins of the man who touches them.

We swam in the river while our clothes hung on the tree branches to dry. We played and sang, *Garwe, herisadza;* Crocodile, here is your sadza. One person was the crocodile and everyone else teased him pretending to give him sadza. The crocodile danced and sang *'swederera'*, get closer, until he pounced on one of us and ran away to eat her. We learnt to swim that way, running away from the 'crocodile'. Naked, we did cartwheels in the river sand. Then we sang and danced on the rocks, swam, rolled in the river sand and jumped in and out of the water. We scrubbed and massaged each other's backs with stones and compared the sizes of our budding breasts. We took *nyungururwi* – the black river insects from the water and got them to bite our nipples. The bites were sharp and painful. They would make our breasts grow big quickly. The more pain we felt, the bigger the breasts would become, though they were only good for breastfeeding. Breasts had nothing to do with sex: bottoms did. Men loved bottoms. Big round bottoms and thick legs. A woman with such assets was not only good *pabonde*. She would give more than enough pleasure to a man. She was also capable of giving birth to many children and her strength in the field was unquestionable.

By sunset we were tired of swimming, our skin was dry and grey; our eyes were red and itchy. So we rubbed ourselves with soap, scrubbed our feet with a stone, rinsed our bodies in a separate upstream pool and lay naked on the rocks to dry. Then we massaged our bodies with peanut oil until we looked clean, smooth and shiny. In the golden glow of the sunset, we carried our water pots home.

At fourteen, Mbuya stopped us from playing the crocodile games in the water. But we could still dance naked on the river rocks to show off our growing bottoms. We were old enough to listen to her and Va-Makumbi tell stories of love, sex, marriage and motherhood. While we lay on the flat rocks Mbuya and VaMakumbi talked about the 'beast' that lies in all men. The 'beast' must never be awakened until a girl is ripe enough for marriage. If you join your pelvis too close to a man, the 'beast' has a habit of waking up very quickly. It rises when a man touches the waist beads. A man must never be allowed to touch your beads, unless you want the 'beast' to bite you.

VaMakumbi sang poetry about the beauty of flowers and petals (labias) between our legs. She instructed us on how to pull the petals to make them longer. This way future games played with the husband before the main act was going to be easier and even more pleasurable. When Mbuya and VaMakumbi were not there, Tete Raina, my father's youngest sister, took over the instructions. She could not do it while Mbuya was around. Mothers and daughters never discussed what to do *pabonde*. Never! My mother did not come down to the river with us. If she did, she always left before the sex talk began. Only a grandmother, an aunt or *tete*, could teach us. Tete Raina showed us the treasures between her legs, long petals and all. She was proud of her ability to please men. *Varoora* teased her endlessly. They said that if she was so good at keeping men happy *pabonde*, how come she had been through two husbands and no child? Why was she back in the village interfering with her brothers' marriages? She should find her own man and become someone's *muroora* in another village. *Varoora* had the license to tell the truth through jokes. Some of what they said really hurt – especially the fact that Tete Raina was infertile. Tete Raina said she was not offended. It was better that they talked about it rather than whisper behind her back. A heavy burden got lighter if it was discussed openly with humour. But the jokes must have bothered her a lot more than she wanted us to know. One day she packed her bags and said she was going to Salisbury to look for work as a housemaid. She came home once a year, on Rhodes and Founders day.

Couples did not demonstrate passion or intimacy in public. They did not kiss or even embrace openly. Night time was the only time husbands and wives got together alone in their respective huts. All day men were out working in the fields or hunting. At evening time they sat with other men at the *dare*, the men's meeting place. The *dare* was for men only where they talked men's affairs. Some of them were busy preparing their iron spears in hot furnaces, *mvuto*, carved stools and axe handles, made fish nets and wove mats and baskets. Sadza from each wife was delivered to them. They tasted dishes from every house and ate together. Every woman's ability to cook was judged by the taste buds of the men at the *dare*. Sometimes we heard much laughter, singing and drinking coming from there. Young men learnt a lot about women from the uncles and grandparents at the *dare* and also at their own bathing place.

When the whole village compound was quiet, Piri and I went from hut to hut listening for the love-making noises. We made bets as to who was going to spot a pregnancy first. Even old men like Sekuru VaDhikisoni had sex. It was village knowledge that Mbuya had chased Sekuru VaDhikisoni out of the *hozi*, the granary floor they used to share long before she claimed old age as the reason for refusing *pabonde* with him. She said he smelt of breast milk because he was spending many long nights in the arms of his breast-feeding young wives. Sekuru VaDhikisoni was not embarrassed by Mbuya's remarks. Much to my pious father's embarrassment, Sekuru openly boasted that he preferred the heat from his younger wives than Mbuya's dry thighs.

Though Mbuya never mentioned the word sex except in metaphors,

Piri and I knew that a person visiting Mbuya's hut before sunrise had a problem to do with sex. She referred to the sex act as a man and a woman joining pelvises together. She had intimate details of most people's sexual lives. Just by looking at them, she could tell how often young women in the village had sex and how soon they would get pregnant. She also knew which one of the cousins or grandsons was infertile. Mbuya removed the shame of infertility from the man by secretly arranging for another one of the brothers or cousins to step in and give the seed to the woman. If the husband knew, he turned a blind eye to it. This way the same genetic seed stayed in the family. Not only that, all the children looked alike and they carried the same totem. Mbuya could cure female infertility, sexual dysfunctions in men and any other diseases related to *pabonde*. It was all very discreet. People came from faraway villages. It was easy to guess the sexual problem of each visitor. A young woman who had been married for more than three years and was showing no bump meant she was infertile. Mbuya advised the infertile woman to accept her young sister or niece as a second wife to bear children for the husband. A pregnant woman visiting Mbuya wanted herbal medicine to insert and relax her vaginal muscles so labour will be less painful. A healthy looking married man with children meant he had a serious recent sexual dysfunction. A man like that stayed in Mbuya's hut for a very long time. We knew that his wife had secretly put medicine in his food to tie his 'beast' as punishment for having an affair with someone else. The wife's medicine was so powerful that the 'beast' did not rise at all when the man went to see his secret lover. But once he got back home *pabonde* with his wife, the 'beast' was fine. Mbuya's concoction easily untied the 'beast'. After two or three visits to Mbuya, we saw the man coming back with a goat as payment for Mbuya's services. This meant the man was in control of his 'beast' at home and also at his lover's place.

I shared the mat with Mbuya in her hut to keep her warm until I was fifteen. Mbuya said it was almost time for marriage. But the missionaries came and said, no, it was time to leave the village and some get Western education. That was the end of sleeping with Mbuya, my grandmother.

We Are All Comrades Now

Fungisayi Sasa

We oppose dynasties and depose kings.
Descend from your throne,
Step out of your gated mansion, remove your designer shoes
And feel the red dust sink into your feet.
You are no better than I,
Communism made us all comrades.
We bow to a common goal.

Comrade Poet Laureate Petros Manhanga (January, 2022)

***

'Hullo.'

'Well, aren't you going to thank me?'

'For what?' Petros could hear her sharp intake of breath. She was clearly offended. Then, silence. She was probably going to scold him for five minutes, and then complain about how nobody appreciated her, especially him. He was glad he'd disabled Skype and video-calling on his android landline. It was going to be a long telephone conversation. He was about to provide an appropriate, seemingly sincere, apology that would soothe her when the housemaid, Chipo, entered.

'Comrade *baas*. The security man is on the video intercom...'

'Chipo, how many times have I told you that you don't have to tell me about the intercom? Just give me the message.'

'Yes, comrade *baas*. The video intercom says there's a big box for you at the gate. Should he let the van driver into the yard?' Chipo stood with her arms folded in front of her.

'A van? I'm not expecting any deliveries.'

'Oooh, your gift has arrived,' his mother squealed over the telephone loud enough for even the housemaid to hear. His mother was still on loudspeaker and Petros had forgotten to place the call on hold.

'I forgive you,' his mother said. 'Don't open it. I will be there in thirty minutes.'

'It's not my birthday...' But she'd already ended the call. Chipo was still standing in front of him, waiting for answer.

'Yes, tell him to let the van in,' Petros told the housemaid, looking past her. He dreaded what his mother had bought him this time. He was still trying to figure out how to return her last present, the house he was living in which she had bought for him when he became Poet Laureate. Despite the fact that he already had a property of his own, she had insisted he sell it and move into the one she had purchased. His mother's time as government minister had given her a taste for luxury and she'd ensured that even after leaving politics her children reaped the benefits of her extravagant tastes. It was no secret how she financed her classy lifestyle: like other ministers in her time, when the government seized the rights to mine the Marange fields, she managed to obtain a steady supply of diamonds that she sold on. She never apologised for her actions but often said, 'In politics, you either eat what is put before you or you go hunting. If you hunt, you might not catch anything so you'll starve. I ate what was put before me.'

***

The Oasis Bar and Grill echoed with the incessant arguments of wealthy men showing off their latest gadgets. Thanks to the newly installed ceiling fans and brighter lights, it was easier to see which shoes, suit or latest accessory a man had without straining one's eyes in the dense cigarette smoke.

'This was made in Japan,' the Minister of Finance, Comrade Steven boasted. He waved his arm at a man standing arms-length behind him. 'Who needs human bodyguards when there are guys like this to be had?

He's made of chrome.'

All eyes turned towards the minister's table and the bolder men, including the bartender, moved closer. Comrade Steven paused, glanced around him carefully, and gently pushed his chair back. He flicked some invisible dust from the right lapel of his Armani suit, opened his arms wide in a welcoming gesture and rose to stand beside the man he'd indicated. Comrade Steven had everyone's attention and he knew it. He smiled, an easy self-assured grin straight out of a Hollywood orthodontist's catalogue.

'He looks real, doesn't he? But he's pure chrome underneath all this artificial skin. He only responds to my voice. He has face recognition technology so he only allows my family members close to me and other individuals whose photos I have entered into his database. Solar-powered so no need to worry when there is a power-cut. He walks, talks, fights, shoots, and plays chess but does not drink, eat, sleep, back-chat, ask me for a raise or sneak into my wife's bed.'

Sycophantic laughter swelled to the ceiling and fell silent as soon as Comrade Steven raised his left hand.

'I'm serious. Isn't this the problem our forefathers had? Garden boys and security guards stealing their wives, their daughters? The scandal, the shame, the unnecessary death of a hardworking employee, the need to look for another wife,' he shook his head. 'Those were sorrowful times but that era does not need to haunt us now. We don't have to repeat our forefathers' mistakes. The future is here, now, in our chrome cousin. He comes with a lifetime guarantee and for those with deep pockets, you can have him custom-made in platinum with gold trimmings and diamonds.'

The men clapped, whistled and those who had been sitting stood up knocking over chairs and drinks. You'd be forgiven for thinking Comrade Steven had just delivered a speech on how to end the dry season and bring an abundance of rain. The bartender and three waiters all lifted the finance minister onto their shoulders. Our Chrome Cousin did not move, obviously their photographs were in his database. Comrade Steven was known to spend more hours at the bar than in his office or at home. He himself claimed that most of his ideas started life as scribbles on an *Oasis Bar* napkin, before they became finance policies influencing the lives of every citizen.

'What about unemployment Steven?' The man spoke softly but everyone heard him.

Comrade Steven frowned, the voice was familiar but he could not quite place it. The crowd of business men parted and the bar staff carried the finance minister, still on their shoulders, to the man who had spoken. He was sitting in a chair by the door and wore a large-brimmed safari hat that hid his face. The man didn't look up when Comrade Steven stood beside him. Our Chrome Cousin waited arm's length behind his master.

'What about unemployment?' The finance minister asked. His tone was not friendly.

'If you purchase more of these tin men, what jobs will be left for the unemployed?'

The finance minister shrugged his lean shoulders and unbuttoned his Armani jacket. Comrade Steven was well known for starting fights and inciting mobs to violence. During his time as a young veteran in the Youth Militia, he had managed to hospitalise seven men, one of whom was his own brother. Blood relations meant nothing to the finance minister when a political advantage was to be gained. Comrade Steven gently eased himself into the chair opposite the man who had spoken to him. He casually leaned forward, took the man's glass of wine and poured out the drink on the floor beside him.

'Unemployment is a careless word to throw around in a nation as prosperous as ours. Only foolish philosophers speak of such things and eventually they die.' Comrade Steven threw the wine glass over the man's head and it smashed on the wall just behind him. The man in the safari hat did not flinch. Comrade Steven stood up quickly buttoned his jacket, turned to his audience with his Hollywood smile and once again opened his arms in a welcoming gesture.

'Bartender, give every man a drink. This round is on me.'

A cheer rose up into the rafters and all the men moved quickly to the bar shouting out their orders.

Comrade Steven leaned in close to the man who had challenged him, 'By the way my bodyguard is not made out of *tin* but *chrome* and it's Comrade Steven to you.'

The man in the safari hat grabbed Comrade Steven's hand, gripped it tightly and twisted slowly. Comrade Steven winced in pain but Our Chrome Cousin did not move.

'I will bear that in mind. Your tin-man can't protect you from me! I am already in his database. Remember that, Comrade.'

The man let go and pushed the finance minister so suddenly that he stumbled backwards to the floor. The man walked out quietly, un-challenged. Everybody else in the bar was so busy enjoying a free drink that they did not notice Comrade Steven lying on the floor while Our Chrome Cousin remained standing at arm's length behind him.

***

'Why, Mother?'

Petros stared at the machine his mother had eagerly unwrapped from its box. He was certain that she'd lost her mind this time.

'It's a work of art isn't it? Platinum with gold detail and diamond eyes for a finishing touch.' She sighed as she clasped Petros' hand and patted his cheek. 'I chose the diamonds myself. Give your mother a kiss and thank her.'

'Why?' Petros had so many whys for this particular moment in time. Why did the bank let her use such a large sum of money? He knew the thing in front of him cost more than his house and car combined. Why didn't she buy it for herself? Why was it wearing Levi's, a Polo shirt and Converse trainers?

'Mother why?' Petros groaned as he lowered himself onto the floor in front of the robot. He sat cross-legged, his head in his hands. He noticed that the mahogany flooring had not been waxed or polished. He would have to talk to Chipo about that again.

'I'm not going to cry,' Petros said firmly.

'Don't be silly,' his mother said patting his head. 'You're so much like your father. Always resorting to theatrics when all you need to say is thank you. Don't you like it?'

Petros could see his mother pacing up and down in front of him, her two-inch heels tapping on the wooden floor. A gentle, rhythmic beat that was steadily increasing in pace. It was a sure warning that he needed to be careful, but the fact was he did not like the robot, and he did not need it.

'You kept the receipt...' he began.

'Receipt!'

His mother's pacing increased and at each sharp turn she left scuff-marks behind her. Petros realised it was going to be a long evening. He'd hoped to rewrite his Independence Day poem and edit the president's speech but he knew he would have to lay aside his plans. His emotional life was potentially at risk and it was crucial that he resolved the matter with the skill of a seasoned negotiator, though when it came to negotiations with his mother, his skills lost a little of their finesse.

'Gifts like this are non-returnable. It's custom-made with a life-time guarantee,' her voice was almost a whisper, but her position intractable, nonetheless.

Her steps quickened to a march. Three short steps, an abrupt stop, a sharp turn and three more short steps. Petros looked out past the robot. The French doors in the living room were open and the heavy scent of jacaranda flowers wafted in on the breeze. The freshly mown grass had developed brown patches and the distant hum of a car engine reminded him that he needed to take his car to the garage for servicing.

'Receipt! My son, have you gone mad?'

Petros sighed resignedly. If he refused her gift, she would give him her usual lecture about how he'd taken advantage of her ever since he was born: From feeding off her breast to asking her to finance his various university qualifications including his doctorate. He had paid back the fees but she would leave that fact out. She had, after all, even called him ungrateful when he deposited the money in her account. How could he make her return this? He knew that as a former minister of the Party, his mother's greatest fulfilment in life was to make other party members envious by lavishing unnecessary gifts on her children, especially her only son. Petros wondered if his mother would be less involved in his life if he married. His future wife would have to be very tolerant or resolutely headstrong, neither quality in this context seemed very appealing.

'What do I need him for?' Petros asked dutifully, submitting to his fate. His mother ceased to clip out a march in her high heels and clapped her hands in delight. She bent forward and kissed his cheek.

'That's all you had to ask my dear son.' She took Petros's hand and he allowed her to help him to his feet. They both stood in front of the robot.

'Well, he can do anything. Don't you need a bodyguard?' His mother asked, hand on her hip.

'Nobody is out to kill me,' Petros replied confidently.

'That's not what I heard,' she said pressing the robot's left eye, 'didn't your last girlfriend try to run you over?'

A gentle whirring sound, not unlike a purr, emitted from the robot.

'That was a misunderstanding,' Petros murmured.

'Twice misunderstood? What about the one before that? What was her name?' His mother pushed in the robot's right eye and a blue laser scanned her finger. The robot beeped twice. 'Getrude. What a name and wasn't she rude! She spray-painted obscenities all over my car when you cancelled a dinner date.'

'Yes, mother but that doesn't mean I need a bodyguard. I just need to choose the right woman.'

'That's the truth. I could have given you an arranged marriage, but you refused. I also suggested virtual dating where you didn't have to meet in person but you could still go out on virtual dates. Too impersonal you said. I set you up on blind dates, the women were too dull, too short, too tall, too shallow and in your own words: hardly the woman a poetic man like myself could engage with at any level let alone marry.'

'She'd taken part in *hondo yeminda* as a teenager, boasted about driving a white farmer off his land with a stolen gun, and she was bald!'

'So?'

'All she talked about was combat and war. She scared me.'

Petros watched his mother as she whispered into the robot's ear.

'Password acknowledged,' the robot spoke. Surprisingly, its voice sounded like that of a narrator on Discovery channel, engaging, but all-knowing. The robot turned its head and looked at him.

'Hello Petros, my name is Peter.' The robot stuck his right hand out.

Petros hesitated.

'Or should I say, "Greetings, Comrade Petros".' The robot saluted sharply and there was the soft chink of platinum hitting platinum, as his right hand hit his forehead and his ankles clinked together. Petros smiled, shaking hands with the robot.

'No, Petros is fine. I'm glad to meet you Peter.'

'See?' Petros' mother said hugging him, gleefully. 'I knew you'd like him. I chose everything they put into Peter's database. He has even read every book and poem you've written. He's an advanced model so he learns new information without you having to upload it into his database. He doesn't simply wait for a command before he does something; he has initiative and robotic intuition. Plus, I showed him photos of all your exes so none of them can come near you as long as he's beside you.'

Petros didn't want to admit it, but he was impressed. Mother had outdone herself.

'He could also help you tidy this house,' his mother said running her finger along the French door. 'Filthy. Look at this dust. What does that housemaid, Chipo, do all day?'

'No *baas*,' Chipo, hearing her name mentioned, ran into the living room door, her bare feet slapping noisily on the wooden floor, leaving slightly moist imprints on the wood. The smell of bleach lingered around her. She pushed past Petros's mother and waved a document in his face. 'I know my rights. The Zimbabwe Garden Boys and Housemaids Union will not accept you firing me without notice. How shall I eat? How will I feed my family? I am going to phone my local union representative right now.'

'See what you have started mother?' Petros muttered. 'Nobody is firing you, Chipo.'

'I would fire you right now for eavesdropping,' his mother said glaring at the housemaid.

'My contract does not say anything about that,' Chipo replied.

'But it does say you need to polish the floors and wipe the windows, doors and window sills at least once every two weeks.' Petros said firmly.

'Once every two weeks. Hah. Who drafted that contract for you? Do you see why my son needs you, Peter?' his mother spoke to the robot as she led him to the leather sofa and turned on the TV. The robot sat beside her and started talking about mankind's need for machines in comparison to their need for domestic help. Petros tried to ignore their conversation and concentrate on Chipo who had taken her mobile phone out of her pocket.

'I'm not firing you. Do you understand?' Petros looked at the clock, it was almost seven. His mother had taken up too much of his time. 'Why don't I drive you home? It's late and I'm sure your family are worried.'

This seemed to calm Chipo who nodded and put her phone back in her pocket. She carefully folded her contract and strode to the kitchen. Petros followed her.

'Mother, I will be back soon. I'm just dropping Chipo home, since you upset her.'

'That girl is spoilt. Very spoilt! Who ever heard of giving the maid a lift when you give her money for transport anyway? So is she going to pay you when you drop her off?' Petros's mother followed him to the kitchen, leaving the robot to watch TV on its own.

Petros took his keys and stepped out the kitchen door. Chipo slung her handbag over her shoulder as she followed him, her head held high. They both got into his car and Petros waved at his mother as she stood at the kitchen door. She waited, watching until the security guard had opened the gate and Petros' solar car had driven out of the yard. Then Petros' mother shut the door and turned off the light. She went into the sitting room, sat beside Peter and turned off the TV.

She looked directly into his diamond eyes, 'Right Peter, let's go over this again. Who is your target?'

The Last Battle

Emmanuel Sigauke

Teacher Elias Gudo scans the room and flinches at the chafed walls and cracked cement floor that have become his nightmare. The room is stale and uninspiring. He didn't like it from the day the headmaster showed it to him. Now, the way things are going, there's no chance that it will be fixed soon, not with the headmaster prioritising the volleyball team's trips to Mutare. He shakes his head, wondering where things went so wrong for him that he landed in this village. Perhaps, if he hadn't shown an interest in writing in secondary school, if the interest hadn't solidified his belief that he was good at English, he wouldn't have taken a teacher training course, and – after the intense two years at Gweru Teacher's College – been deployed to Rusitu Valley. He wants a decent room, even a whole house. But what does the headmaster say? You're single, and as long as you stay single, you can only inhabit one room.

'And, besides, Mr Gudo, a room is a room,' said the headmaster. 'You ought to thank your ancestors that we have electricity and running water. How many rural schools have such luxuries?'

'I need a bigger room, Sir,' he said. 'Is that too much to ask?'

The headmaster shook his head and said, 'You don't have furniture, not even a wooden stool. What do you need a bigger room for, Mister?' 'I'd have it if I had enough space,' Elias rejoined, realising that he'd just lied to himself. Furniture, beds, and shelves required money. When had he last handled that? The headmaster gave him a look that seemed to say, 'Don't kid yourself!'

In the four months he has worked as a new teacher, his first salary hasn't been processed. Money, real money, to afford even the basics – when will he get some? He pauses: 'getting some' doesn't only apply to money. The thought of Tambu gnaws at him, as if not having money equals not having Tambu; to think that she hasn't even bothered to visit him takes his breath away. No wonder teachers turn to students... and, as for them, no he doesn't want to get himself into more trouble than he's bargained for. Still, there is that Form 2 girl, with a body too big for her age, and how she distracts him from teaching with her juicy stare. Little sexy minx! He swats the thought away, remembering Mike, his former college roommate who committed suicide after he impregnated a Form 3 student in Ngorima. Right now, Elias just wants to kill something that deserves to die – roaches – delete them like stubborn words on a page begging to carry a life-changing story.

His room is in a three-bedroom house, occupied by four other teachers, two of whom are sisters, who share the biggest bedroom. To Elias, this is a waste. Perhaps if he had a better room, he might entice one of them to hang out with him... and one thing might lead to another. The sisters are nearly twins, close as they are to each other in age; though the General Science teacher is darker, and he likes dark. The lighter one, the Shona teacher, is too short, but she's still a lot of woman. And she knows it, making Shona jokes in the staff room; jokes from Shona praise poetry: husband and wife thanking each other after love-making – *thank you the one from Guruuswa, you who dodged this and that and pierced here and there until you found your way and ruled where ruling was needed.* She should just become a comedian and entertain Zimbabwe. At least, she receives a salary. They both do, the sisters.

Elias has long set up his kitchen in a corner of his room. He tried to use the community kitchen, hoping to enjoy sharing the space with his colleagues, talking with the sisters, greeting the wife of the teacher whose family occupies two bedrooms, but he was never able to cook, the burners were always occupied. Besides, what had seemed like an opportunity to socialise turned out to be toxic gossiping. The sisters even expected him to take sides, so he decided he was better off alone. The idea of the house, as community, in which teachers can relax after work, felt like the setting of a horror story. Isolation is the best solution. Peace and quiet... only there isn't much peace with this invasion of roaches.

He stretches his muscles and performs some push-ups, to build strength for the fight. His goal is sixty, but he stops at ten. He wrings his hands angrily, the betrayal of the body. He should be fitter than this, be more the warrior he imagines. So he continues, with more determination, and completes another ten, but falls flat on the floor. He resumes. Twenty-one, twenty-two, twenty-three... then, his arms give in, his body quivers from the exertion. Sweat pours from him and his heart plays a drum in his chest.

He walks towards the clothesline for a towel, but a movement near a pile of exercise books catches his attention. Just the thought that they hide in the crevices of his room infuriates him. They're everywhere, even in his folded blankets, textbooks, his novels, and his plates and pots. They rouse him from sleep, especially on nights before he's scheduled to teach Form 4F, a chaotic class which makes a mockery of the teaching profession. He thinks that sometimes the roaches play a Kafka on him and morph into his 4F students, to haunt him in human form. But today he will teach them a lesson.

His eyes rest on his stereo. He kneels beside it and pats its cassette decker. 'Don't worry buddy, we'll terminate the brutes today.' The poor stereo is choking with them. He wonders if they're drawn to take up occupation by the music or the warmth. Maybe they want to listen up close to Voice of America, the only radio channel that Rusitu receives regularly. Don't they have radios where they come from? Their own Voice of Roachland?

He tiptoes away from the stereo, towards his heap of shoes. His loafers, with their flat, hard soles, are effective weapons, but his slippers are even better. Or one of his kitchen utensils, like his *mugoti*? But that would be pure insanity, using the cooking spot to kills roaches. Why spoil something so valuable – that is, if he ever plans to cook again.

Maybe his Oxford Advanced Dictionary. It's heavy enough to grind whole armies at once. But like the smart sane teacher he thinks he is, he decides no. The dictionary is partially responsible for his career choice though if he hadn't crammed it so well, back in Mazvihwa, helping his friends write English letters to girls (*Time and ability have afforded me opportunity to indite this missive...*); if he hadn't fallen in love with words, reading the dictionary from A to Z, he might perhaps have ended in another field, electrical engineering, zoology. But it was that Form 3 teacher, the British expat, a student of social anthropology, who confirmed to him that he was good at the language and gave him his first Oxford Learner's Dictionary. He pictures the dictionary dropping like a nuclear bomb, with that *pha-a-pwaka* that will send juices squirting. Stains... the end of life...

He smiles at the prospect of conquest. But what's he to conquer, the roaches or the dictionary? No, he wants to keep the dictionary clean. Indeed, he wants to keep it forever, into posterity, all its pages intact. This dictionary, this hive of sweet and bitter memories, of the Vonais and Shamisos it helped him win, and the fame, oh the fame. He hears another sound behind his suitcase. The buggers! They should stay away from his suitcase. They mock him by shitting in his shirts. It's not as if the clothes, though not always washed, are dirty. Even if they were, that doesn't give the roaches the right to infest them. Their sense of entitlement irks him; it's like the people in government entitling themselves to his money.

Maybe if he were to stop cooking for a week or two, the creatures would lick their supplies dry and leave him alone. But, who's he kidding? Where else would he eat? Not at the Ndakopa restaurant. Where would he find that kind of money?

Another sound from the mealie-meal bag. 'Enough!' he shouts. 'Let's thicken this plot now. I'll show you who's boss.' He closes the curtain to darken the room, and remains still for a moment, to avoid alerting them. After five long minutes, he switches on the light and notices two fatties crawling up the wall. He grabs a flip-flop, dives and releases a slap that reduces one to a stain. The other struggles upwards and spreads its grease-covered wings. A whole week's foray among the dirty dishes has fattened it, so its efforts to fly provide a comic spectacle. He kills it instantly and stares at the two stains, shakes his head, and laughs. The laughter feels good, a cup of water after a scorching afternoon in the field. He remembers those hot days in Mototi when he and his Maiguru toiled on the land, his sister-in-law always reminding him to work hard, saying, 'This is the only way we can afford to send you to school. Once you're done, you will never have to worry.' *Right, I'll never have to worry! Thanks a bunch, Maiguru MaSibanda.* He shakes his head, to ward off memories like this. But another takes him to a hot afternoon at Gweru Teacher's College library, another kind of field, where he studied for more than eight hours, alternating poetry penning with Shakespeare cramming, while his friends were having fun downtown. Gweru was a kind of alternative field, after the university failed to admit him... when he didn't get enough points at A-Level to study law, or English, or Shona, or Divinity. He starts shaking, from a deep, gnawing pain, which quickly turns to anger and makes him want to smash the stereo, his dear stereo. Images of wilting maize and millet fields flit through his mind. But he laughs and Maiguru laughs with him, laughing, as she used to say, in celebration of poverty as if it was wealth; and now, these small crops, these stains on the walls, and the lifeless shells on the floor, his harvest. Maybe, he too is destined to end up no more than a blot in the universe. But he's a fighter – that's how he managed to pass O-Level, proceeded to A-Level, and to college. Not many in Mazvihwa made it beyond those fields and the hills. He imagines them still toiling in that arid land, with no dreams of becoming anything beyond farmer or fisherman. He laughs, unsure this time whether he's laughing at the stains on the wall, or at his peers in Mazvihwa.

Another roach makes a dash from the stove and threads its way towards his books. If it moves in a straight line, the first book it will reach is *Black Sunlight*, just below *House of Hunger*, above which is *A Grain of Wheat*. He was reading them simultaneously yesterday, reading them like a writer, examining style, or the strings that tie each story together, but he gave up as the exercise led nowhere; not with all the thoughts about his salary and food.

The roach races to the wall. When it begins to climb, Elias unleashes a blow that catches its rear, and it falls into a basin of sugar. How disgusting! The nasty thief! He scoops out the creature with a spoon and dumps it on the floor. Then he slaps.

A lot more are in hiding, watching him, perhaps even laughing at him. The mealie-meal bag is another haunt of theirs. They spend days filling up their bellies there, and he often finds them lying unconscious, a way of vacationing, perhaps? A rehearsal of death?

He grabs the bag by the neck, strangling it, lifts and sits it in the middle of the floor. The top layer of the meal is coated with struggling, ashen chaos. A few try to climb out, but fall back in. He bought this bag with borrowed money. Now they sit on his food, just as someone is sitting, or shitting, on his money at the Salary Services Bureau. What's taking them so long? Do they know what it means to be stuck in this remote valley? Of course not. Who, sitting in those Harare offices and sipping tea all day, would worry about a teacher at Ndima Secondary?

'Fine, I'll hit the hell out of you,' he tells them. The roaches jump about like popping corn, but he cannot release them; they are his catch, the prize of his teacher training.

He should just throw away the polluted meal. Throw the whole bag into the trash pit outside. 'NDIMA TEACHER STARVES TO DEATH'. He can see the headline in the *Manica Post*. That useless education ministry, and the lazy headmaster, would be happy.

He starts towards the door, but stops, shakes his head. The floor soon becomes a mess of white and brown as he slaps and stomps. The roaches struggle, but some are squashed. Elias wants to show them that they cannot get too comfortable in his room. He squashes more, allowing only a few to crawl away, injured. Eventually, these will die too, or their injuries will serve as a warning to others back home.

Only if he taught in town, he wouldn't have to deal with this crap. There, the authorities wouldn't forget his existence. Any delay in his salary and he would be down at the Salary Services Bureau downtown, creating a scene. But that is if he taught in Harare, at Highfield High, anywhere but in this valley, where heavy rain causes landslides which have blocked the roads, and nothing is coming through: newspapers, food, love-letters, pay-cheques.

The roaches have formed a snakelike rope that has begun to wriggle up the wall. How can there be so many of them? He dives and strikes at the head of the snake. They fall back on the floor and he stomps on them. *They* should give him his salary! *They* should make the rains stop! They should give him a better room, a whole house even. *They* should understand how difficult life has become in Zimbabwe. Juices squirt in all directions, some landing on his lower lips. He can taste the saltiness, the disgusting guts.

He moves utensils to expose those underneath. Beneath a pot he finds three fat and shiny ones. Two escape immediately, leaving behind a slow-moving elder with a bulging belly. 'They have potbellies too. I bet this one is a cabinet minister. Die, you corrupt idiot!' The politician explodes and the juices of stolen wealth fly in all directions. He attacks the wall and the new mess from unsuspecting escapees smears his hands. These were thugs too, perhaps Minister and Deputy Minister of Education.

He's tired of their looting; he hates the way they mock him, how they wave beer bottles and laugh at him when he asks for a swig. Buy your own, they seem to say, then they collapse with laughter when they realise that buying is not part of his vocabulary. They even show off their lovers and expose wads of money.

He doesn't want to be reminded of Tambu. All those things she said, the last time they were together.

'You look like a goat herder,' she said.

'You're just joking, right?'

'Perhaps in your dreams I'm kidding.' She dodged Elias's passion-filled hand.

'What's wrong, honey?' he said, not knowing what else to say.

'You, you're what's wrong."

For a moment he heard her words as a tease, moved closer, remembering the moves that used to lock her in passion.

'Stop that!' she said, pushing him away.

He froze as the sharpness of her voice cut through his conscience.

'You need to stop honeying me too. I'm not your honcy, understand?'

Her lips quivered when she said that damaging word, 'understand'. It didn't seek the understanding of the listener because there was nothing to understand. But he wanted to keep on trying, to see if trying was too late in their relationship. 'But, seriously, is this necessary?'

To his surprise, she wanted to say more, and he listened, but from a safe, respectful distance.

'You know what you did – and didn't do, but let's start with what you did.' She drew closer to him. 'We had an agreement.' She moved back. 'What happened to Mutare? Urban schools, remember?'

Oh, so this was what she was acting up about? He licked his lips, getting ready to clarify everything, summarily. 'What choice did I have?' he said, but sensed that even what he was about to say wouldn't work, but he said it anyway. 'Should I have said 'no' when they deployed me to the only place they could find me a post?' He paced around, bothered by the ineffectiveness of his delivery. He should have said something more romantic, something reassuring. 'So until a city job comes through, I'm stuck in Rusitu.' He raised his voice. 'You think it's easy for me?'

'So a town job will just come on its own without you looking for it, saying, "Hey, Elias, I'm here!"?' She twisted her lips as if she was in pain. Elias realised then how serious she was.

'I'm sorry that the place is remote, but understand...'

'Understand what?'

'There are people there too.' He paused, thinking about those people. 'A whole world of people who need educators like me.'

She coughed out a laugh. '*Educators like me...;* you can educate all you want.'

'What's that tone for?' He thought she had gone too far, mimicking him like that. In case she had forgotten, he had trained for this career.

'Live with your 'people' and stop bothering me.' She started walking away. 'Don't try to contact me again.'

He didn't want her to have the last say. 'You know it doesn't take that long for them to process the pay,' he said, soon realising the stupidity of his words. 'I know they will pay me one day,' he paused, 'I just know they will.'

She stopped and tilted her head, waiting to hear more. Nothing came, so she resumed walking with a slight sway of the hips. 'You were supposed to transfer just after a few weeks, once you were in the system. Come up with an emergency, a reason to be in town, taking care of some relative, anybody, make up stuff, but three month later you're still in the back of beyond.'

'It's not that easy,' he said. 'So in your head you think I like being in the village?' He paused, deciding if that made sense. 'Do you think I don't want to teach in the city with you?'

'It doesn't matter. The engagement party never happened, and you sure don't seem to understand the meaning of the word "commitment".' She frowned. 'Or maybe that's something you village types don't know? Engagements and such?'

'What?' He felt a wave of anger, but he wanted to remain calm.

'Don't waste your time,' she said. 'I've moved on.'

He opened his mouth but no words came out.

'Sorry, Elias. I have standards and I am a human, not a log.' Then she walked away, leaving him standing confused on the sidewalk.

He shakes off a dizzy sensation as he spots a tiny female sauntering towards the door. He kneels and looks at it. 'So what do I get, heh? You're too thin, yet your people steal my food.' But the slim girl moves on, uncaring. He insists, 'Tell me, what do I get out of it?' He looks up at the roof, then back at the female. 'You were lucky to find a job in Mutare. Did you sleep with someone at the ministry?' He feels tears in his eyes. 'So you found someone, heh?' The female roach slides away. No, he can't let her go. He pursues her. 'Talk to me!' he shouts, but what can she say? Tell him to leave her alone, that she has moved on, has found someone? 'So who is it? An Education Officer, someone's husband? Talk to me!' But she crawls to safety. He's not letting her abandon him. Whack! He's killed his darling.

He lifts a skillet, exposing a dozen that appear to be napping, shiny, brown-winged youths and pregnant, wingless mothers. Abdomens extended, egg cases protruding like missiles ready to launch, they wave their antennae leisurely. The young seem to whisper to the old, and each member of the group moves closer to the nearest pregnant female. It's like a ritual, perhaps a prelude to a massive birth. And they multiply! If they were dollars, he would be the Bill Gates of Zimbabwe. But these are thieves; they want him to remain poor, yet expect him to work, teach their children. The community continues its feast, ignoring him completely. He can just imagine the horrible things they're saying about him; he can even hear their jeers, and when he sees a svelte youth spread her wings, he is seized by ire. He grinds the colony with his bare foot, stops and sighs victoriously, but his triumph crumbles when he sees another group crawling towards the stove. The pan hits the floor with an ear-splitting sound.

'Jesus!' he shouts, when he notices the damage to the implement. 'I borrowed you from Maiguru. She'll kill me.' He looks at it and then at the spot it hit, where startled roaches race for their lives, and are joined by others fleeing from their previously quiet neighbourhoods. One part of the wall is now coated with brown life as another mass advances to the roof.

He arms himself with two shoes. If they think they can escape from him, they're dreaming. He scampers forward, staggers, nearly slips, but he regains his balance and starts beating at the ones on the wall. He and his shoes have become one weapon, a machine eating into this wall of enemies. Everything on the way, everything that has or has not asked for trouble, all these students, all these other teachers, the family in the adjoining room; he grinds them all to death. He stops to catch his breath and to wipe sweat from his face. But why stop? Why bother wiping sweat. He takes off his T-shirt instead, attacks again.

'Why do you keep coming back?' he asks as he paints the wall with guts. 'Why don't you go to your headmaster's house?' He looks around and shakes his head. 'No, I don't have a mess here. I'm a clean man, trained the right way at college, cleanliness, etiquette.' And he starts laughing, thinking, *cleanliness, my ass.* Laughing and laughing, taking a break from grinding. Laughing and thinking, about what other weapon to use. He can wrestle with them, and if that fails, there is karate, there is Kung Fu.

Now he has a million arms like pistons, ejectors of decimating poison. The roaches attack, so he kicks and flails. He kicks everything in the way: pots, books, a sugar basin and salt shaker, mugs, plates. He throws a shoe at the window, but really it's a missile launching. Another at the door, where someone knocked, paused, knocked and went away. A metal tea-cup sitting in the middle of the floor is kicked until it careens and hits the window frame. When it falls on the floor it wails. 'Shut up, you idiot! Go tell your headmaster you're hungry.' He gives it another kick, but the pain cuts through his bare foot. He dances and limps back to the war zone, thinking, I'm all right, no, I'm not, yes I am.

He rips clothes off hangers and scatters them on the floor. 'Be good for something, you lazy bastards!' He picks up a jacket, spreads it like a net. 'Help me capture these thieves! Take that corner, you blasted shirt, watch the door. You patched pair of jeans, squash from the middle.' He throws the jacket back on the heap and stomps on the clothes.

He opens a cardboard box of food and sees that they've arranged themselves like a defence line, coating the inside. He starts shaking. 'I'm not crazy! I'm a loafer. I'm a soldier!' Satisfied with the sound of his voice, which registers normality, he stares at the embattled layer of cockroaches. He wants to burn the box, and what little food it contains. Or just take the box to the headmaster's house, say, 'Here are the goblins you sent to kill me!' He will stand there and laugh as they chew up the headmaster.

Or burn the box here. Pour paraffin over it. Strike a match. He smiles as he imagines the whole house catching fire, then the whole school. He fumbles for a match, and when he finds it near the stove, he takes a paraffin container and returns to the box. The roaches inside don't move; it's as if they're ready for the end. 'I'm ready too,' he whispers at them. 'I was ready before you were born.' He laughs. 'But some of you were born last week!' The roaches don't care. This is their kingdom.

Now he's begging them to allow him to join them.

Their king laughs at him. His bodyguards move forward, but the king tells them to move back, and he stands up and beckons Elias closer, as if he's going to embrace him.

Elias stretches out his arms, grins.

'And,' begins the king, who is draped in animal fur, 'what gives you the guts, fool?'

'I'm one of you!' Elias says. 'My ancestors lived here before, worked for you for centuries.'

The roaches laugh.

'Give me asylum, precious king,' he says, falling on his knees.

'You're a dreamer,' says the king, sipping Scotch.

'No, *mambo wangu*, I'm your loyal soldier.' He reveals his assegai. 'Let me stay.'

The king laughs again, rolling on the ground, the others coiling around him. Then the king untangles himself and sits on his golden stool. He looks at Teacher Elias Gudo. 'You don't even get paid for what you do, what makes you think you could be a productive member of this kingdom?'

'Just give me a chance. Let me live here.'

'You can't.'

'Oh yes, I can.'

'Try it!' The king summons warriors.

'Watch me.'

He strikes a match and tilts he paraffin container. He wants it to suck in the flame first like a chameleon gulping a fly. A tongue of fire will form and consume the room, then the whole house, soon spreading to the other houses, and then the classroom blocks. His heart beats faster. His eyes lose focus, and his mind goes blank, the way he wants it now: no thought, no weight.